T E
A
APOCRYPHA
in
Limerick Verse

THE
OLD
TESTAMENT
AND THE
APOCRYPHA
in
Limerick Verse

CHRISTOPHER

GOODWINS

John Hunt
Publishing Limited

Copyright © 2002 John Hunt Publishing Ltd
Text © 2001 Christopher Goodwins

ISBN 1 84298 019 X

Designed by Jim Weaver Design

Write to:
John Hunt Publishing Ltd
46A West Street
Alresford
Hampshire SO24 9AU
UK

A CIP catalogue record for this book is available
from the British Library.

Printed in Guernsey, Channel Islands

CONTENTS

Contents

Apocrypha

About this book

After seeing *The New Testament in Limerick Verse* many people suggested that the Old Testament and the Apocrypha should also be published in the same sort of format.

What follows here is by no means perfect, but it does attempt to include the major themes and personalities of the Old Testament and the Apocrypha.

It has the same aim – to encourage people to read the real thing. If not – and if this is the only work that people ever read – then at least they will have gleaned a flavour of what the Old Testament and the Apocrypha are about.

I can visualise people waiting in hotels or airport lounges for a connection in about three hours' time, having nothing to occupy their minds. If they were to see this book, I reckon that they would read it very easily – from cover to cover!

I can see it being really helpful to teachers, faced with a fourth-year class taking RE as the last period on a Friday afternoon in the heat of summer.

I can envisage it lying around in doctors' and dentists' waiting rooms.

This book could be of enormous help to clergy, in Confirmation preparation, or to people who have shied away from church, simply because some worship seems to be so dauntingly complicated and wordy.

The good thing about it is that much of the Old Testament provided the Scriptures that helped to form the mind of Jesus. And, as St. Paul said, '*Have this mind in you, which was also in Christ Jesus!*' (Phil.2: 5) – and this is the motivation behind the work.

Yes – I know that some of the rhymes have been stretched to the limits, in order to make the rhythm fit better – but, as nobody has ever done this exercise before, then hopefully it's better than nothing!

I would like to thank Peter Wright, priest, for his encouragement and constructive criticism. He was the only person at my theological college who had the ability to inspire me to get excited about the Bible!

Finally, I would like to thank my wife, Doreen, for putting up with my single-minded determination to get the work completed, and for her patience in checking it, over and over again!

I hope it encourages you to read the real thing!

CHRISTOPHER GOODWINS
Isleham, August 2001

THE OLD TESTAMENT

Genesis 1: 1

If you want to know how we began
The clues are in Genesis, man!
There was nothing at first
Till the universe burst
On infinity, as God's plan.

Genesis 1: 2

To understand life, it seems right
That God made the lot – day and night!
The universe grew
As His Spirit moved too!
It was good, as things came to the Light!

Genesis 2: 18–24

The intricate parts took their places
Right up to the first human races.
Whoever they were
Eve and Adam infer
God created us from the same faces.

GENESIS 3

With everything beautiful there
Temptation was too great to bear.
The fruit of the tree
Gave them knowledge, you see –
Choosing evil or good. It was fair!

GENESIS 3: 1–6

Along came the serpent. 'Don't wait!
You may eat the fruit, so I state!'
It did look so nice,
And it just took a trice!
The damage was done! They both ate!

GENESIS 3: 7–10

But then, in the cool of the day
They both heard the voice of God say –
'Where are you, you two?'
'We were naked, and threw
Some fig leaves on, and hid away!'

GENESIS 3: 11–13

'But how did you know you were bare?'
Asked God. 'Have you eaten fruit where
I told you not to?'
'Oh – the serpent said You
Wouldn't mind! We accepted the dare!'

GENESIS 3: 14–19

'Well, now you must pay for your sin!
These clothes are for you to get in!
And so you must toil
As you till all the soil,
And dust unto dust will begin!'

GENESIS 3: 24

So that spelt the end of the fun –
Though creation had just begun!
Hence Adam and Eve
Had, from Eden, to leave!
And this is how 'The Fall' was done!

GENESIS 4: 1-4

Yes – Adam and Eve had the two
Sons. Cain was the first, the one who
Was a tiller of soil
Who, with sweat and with toil
Did rather successfully, too!

GENESIS 4: 2

Their second son, Abel, was deep
Into keeping farm animals – sheep.
Their friendship fell out
When Cain began to shout
At Abel, and that made him weep.

GENESIS 4: 3-6

Cain offered his first fruits, and said
'*Accept this, Lord!*' But God instead
Accepted the other
Which came from his brother –
Which made Cain wish Abel were dead!

GENESIS 4: 8–9

Cain took it into his own head
That Abel would be better dead.
He slew him one day,
When God questioned him. 'Hey –
I'm not Abel's keeper!' he said!

GENESIS 4: 10–13

The Lord said, 'Where's Abel? Tell me!'
But Cain's guilty secret, you see
Was there to be found
In the blood on the ground.
Thus Cain became fugitive, he!

GENESIS 4: 14–16

So Cain was marked out by the Lord
Who vowed that when Cain went abroad
Whoever might find him
Should kill him, or wound him,
Hence eastward Cain fled, towards Nod.

GENESIS 4: 19–22

Lamech had kids, three or four
Like Jabal, the cattle man, or
Jubal, musician,
And Tubal-Cain – fission
Was his skill, with metals galore.

GENESIS 6: 13–22

On earth families spread like wild fire
And some ignored God. *'Why enquire
What happens if we
Get too clever?'* *'You'll see!'*
Said God, as the rain became dire.

GENESIS 6

One family planted its trust
Very firmly in God. *'If we must,'*
Said Noah, *'We'll go build
A boat – and not get killed
By floodwaters!'* – He had it sussed!

GENESIS 7

The others stood by and just jeered
At Noah, who waved back – and cheered
When the flood drowned the baddies –
But not lass or laddies,
Nor wife nor his family! How weird!

GENESIS 7: 14–16

He'd taken on board all he could
Of all living creatures who would
Get into the ark
Not afraid of the dark!
Including a raven. That's good!

GENESIS 8

As God made His point, the rain stopped,
And onto Mount Ararat dropped
The ark. All within it
Cried, '*Praise God! We've done it!*'
And onto dry land out they popped!

GENESIS 8: 8

A year had passed by, when a dove
Flew out on a mission. *'My love,'*
Noah said to his missus,
'This bird' – between kisses –
'Will come back with hope from above!'

GENESIS 8: 11

The olive branch, quite fresh and green
For twelve months had never been seen.
'This means we are saved!'
Noah said, and he raved
With excitement. *'Trust God! – God I mean!'*

GENESIS 9: 1–17

The rainbow had signalled God's end
To flooding. So now they could send
The whole boatload out.
'No more rain!' God said. *'Nowt! –*
It's a promise I'll always defend!'

GENESIS 9: 18-28

Lived rather a long time, did Noah.
He had only three sons, not four.
Shem and brother Ham
And then Japeth. Yes, Ma'am!
These ones were his family. Oh, coo er!

GENESIS 10

'Go, multiply!' – God said, 'and bud,
But Noah – watch out for the mud!
They numbered so many
Became two a penny –
The ones who'd survived from the flood.

GENESIS 11: 1-5

At that time, they all spoke the same.
They got on quite well, but became
So greedy for power
That they each built a tower.
The higher, the greater their fame!

GENESIS 11: 6–9

God saw through their pride and their plots.
One language He turned into lots.
They suddenly saw
That their power was no more –
And their babbling was just like a tot's!

GENESIS 11: 29

Abram went out and got married
To Sarai. Both of them tarried
In Ur, till God said
'It is time that you led
All the family to Canaan!' He hurried.

GENESIS 12: 1–3

Said God, *'You'll do just what I say!'*
Abram said, *'Lord – there's no other way!'*
'OK, then! That's fine
All your blessings are mine!'
So the nation emerged, day by day.

GENESIS 12: 6–7

At Shechem, Abe heard the Lord say
'I'll give you this land here, one day!'
He then built an altar.
And faith did not falter
As Abram then went on his way.

GENESIS 12: 7–11

God promised that one day He would
Give Abram his own land for good.
But now, south he went
Into Egypt as sent
Where a famine was raging. No food!

GENESIS 12: 14–20

The Pharaoh of Egypt showed lust
For Abram's wife. He was nonplussed
When God sent a plague!
He could not now renege –
As Abram then set off in trust.

GENESIS 13: 1–18

With Sarai and brother Lot
Abe went south, and so soon forgot
The past. Then at Mamre
An altar built. '*Hey we*
By far prefer this building plot!'

GENESIS 13:8–10

Abe said, with a commanding voice
To Lot, '*You go left. That's your choice!*
And I'll take the right!
So I bid you goodnight!'
And they parted, amidst lots of noise.

GENESIS 13: 11–18

So Lot chose the Jordan plain east,
Abram chose Canaan. The least
He could do was to say
'*I'm so glad I'm this way!*
Build an altar! And let's have a feast!'

GENESIS 14: 11–24

Poor Lot had a really rough time,
And got caught in battle and slime.
To the rescue came Abie
Saved Lot, brother, baby.
Melchizedek blessed him in rhyme.

GENESIS 15: 1–4

At that stage, poor Abe had no heir.
He, Sarai, both near despair!
But God had a plan
For this patriarch man.
'Believe me, Abe!' God said. So there!

GENESIS 15: 5–17

'Your family will be as the stars –
So great in a very few years!'
'How can I believe it?'
Said Abie, 'I've planned it!'
Said God, 'You can drop all your fears!'

GENESIS 16

'Your future depends on a girl –
A maid, who's called Hagar, will hurl
Herself in your life
She'll be your second wife.'
Bore Ishmael, fair-haired, with curl.

GENESIS 17: 1–8

This Covenant came into force
And Abram replied, almost hoarse,
'I'll never forsake You
Dear God, I will take You!'
'OK, Abraham! Yes, of course!'

GENESIS 17: 9–14

'There's one thing I want you to do,'
Said God, 'And it's all up to you!
Just circumcise men
Eight days old, please, and then
It marks you as mine! Yes – it's true!'

GENESIS 17: 15–19

'Your Sarai's Sarah from now
And she'll be a mummy too!' 'How?'
Asked Abie. 'We're old!'
'Oh – you just won't be told!'
Scolded God. 'Have more faith!' – Wow, oh wow!

GENESIS 18: 1–15

Then Sarah, she overheard this,
And laughed till she cried! 'I'm a Miss –
And I'm far too decrepid
For motherhood!' Tepid
Remark, but gave Abie a kiss.

GENESIS 19: 1–26

'There's one thing you must not do – not!
In Sodom the men want you, Lot!
But quit there for Zoar
Don't look back, but go! – Er –
Bad news! Your wife's now become salt!'

GENESIS 19: 30–38

That night, Lot drank far too much wine.
His daughter lay with him till nine.
The other one too –
Well aware what he'd do!
'Now Moab and Ammon are thine!'

GENESIS 21: 1–4

Old Sarah conceived, had a child –
Delighted her Abraham wild!
He took a sharp knife
As he said to his wife
'God marks Isaac now, undefiled.'

GENESIS 21: 9–21

But trouble blew up in Abe's camp
When Hagar, his Gyppie-slave vamp
Started mocking poor Sarah
She tore out her hair-a
'You've got to get rid of that tramp!'

16

GENESIS 22: 1–3

God now put old Abe to the test.
'Your son, Isaac, has to go west!
So, like a young goat
Put a knife to his throat
And slay him, so you may be blessed!'

GENESIS 22: 4–13

Thus Abraham did as God said
His knife poised to kill Isaac dead –
When God changed His mind:
'You've such faith! Look behind!
There's a ram in the hedge. Him instead!'

GENESIS 22: 14–19

So God had led Abe to the brink,
But at the last moment, said 'Think
Of the pact we have made!
So Abe, don't be afraid!
It's for ever! A Covenant-link!'

GENESIS 23

Sarah, a hundred two seven
Departed this life. Went to heaven.
In Machpelah cave
Abie made Sarah's grave
At Mamre (that's Hebron), Canaan.

GENESIS 24: 1–15

Abe sent off his servant to look
For a wife his son Isaac could hook.
At Nahor he found one
Rebekah, a sound one,
A girl who would make a great cook!

GENESIS 24: 16–67

As the dowry changed hands, so she went
With Abe's servant, camels and tent.
Isaac knelt there and prayed
Till he saw the parade,
And 'Becky,' for whom he had sent.

GENESIS 25: 1–10

Abraham married again
And his family increased by the ten.
Then to Isaac, gave all
But Abe died in the Fall.
And was buried at Machpelah plain.

GENESIS 25: 11–26

Abe's two-handled family thrived.
And dozens of children survived!
Rebekah bore twins
But remarked, amidst grins
'*Rough and smooth, Isaac dear!*' Uncontrived!

GENESIS 25: 27–28

Ike's favourite twin, hairy Esau
Liked hunting. While Jacob his twin bro'
Was Rebekah's pet,
Preferred home life. But yet
There were problems afoot. You know who for!

GENESIS 25: 29–34

Now Jacob had hunted all day
And dinner was ready. Hey, hey!
Quite faint, Esau traded
His birthright, and faded
Away, leaving Jacob to play!

GENESIS 26

As Isaac's prosperity grew
So God became close to him. True!
He made friends with all
But his eyesight did pall
Till he no longer knew who was who!

GENESIS 27: 1–26

Rebekah had hatched up a plot
To fool Isaac over a pot
Of stew she had cooked.
Camouflaged so it looked
Like Jacob was Esau. He's not!

GENESIS 27: 27–46

So Jacob received his dad's blessing
But Esau was livid. No messing!
The plot came to light
And he vowed he just might
Kill his brother! Blow Jacob's caressing!

GENESIS 28: 10–12

So Jacob succeeded by guile
Obtaining dad's blessing, but while
He dreamed at Bethel
Of a ladder, which fell
From heaven to earth – mile on mile!

GENESIS 28: 13–22

The angels were up and then down
The ladder from 'Top of the Town'.
'I'm Abraham's God,'
God said, 'and Isaac's!' – Nod
If I'm Yours, too, dear Jacob! Don't frown!'

Genesis 29: 16–18

Laban's two daughters were Leah
And Rachel. Then Jacob came near.
'I'll work seven years
For your Rachel! I'm hers!'
Laban had another idea!

Genesis 29: 19–35

On Jacob, Laban played a trick!
Jake married the wrong daughter. *'Quick –*
I'll serve seven years
More, if I can be hers –
Your Rachel!' The whole joke was sick!

Genesis 30: 22–24

Eventually, Rachel conceived
And Joseph was born. She believed
That God heard her prayer
And allowed her to bear
A son. She was no longer peeved!

GENESIS 32: 22–30

All night Jacob wrestled in vain
But God pricked his conscience again.
'From now on, your name
Will be Israel. A shame
That your hip has been put to such strain!'

GENESIS 35: 9–15

'I'll say this to you just once more,'
God said to young Jacob – 'Encore
It's Israel – your name –
You'll achieve such great fame!
Your kingdom will grow by the score!'

GENESIS 37: 3–4

Joseph was Jacob's young son.
He made him a coloured coat, one
Which made him stand out,
Made his brothers all pout
With such envy. 'Twas no longer fun!

GENESIS 37: 5–10

It didn't help when Joseph dreamed
That wheat and cows, sun and moon, deemed
To fall down before him:
'*Your brothers – ignore them!*'
Was what Joseph's message had seemed.

GENESIS 37: 12–28

Directly to Shechem they raced.
The flock needed feeding, in haste.
Their devious plan
Was to sell Joseph, man!
Then say he was dead! Such bad taste!

GENESIS 37: 31

His coat they threw into a pit
With blood on, so folk would think it
Was where Joseph died.
Its bright colours outside
Would signal Jo's death quite a bit!

GENESIS 37: 32–34

They brought the coat back to his dad.
'Look what has become of the lad!'
They said, between tears
Making Jacob's worst fears
Believe Jo was dead! Jake went mad!

GENESIS 37: 36

But Joseph was safe in the hand
Of the Midianites' travelling band.
To Egypt they came
And sold Joseph – the same –
To Potiphar, Pharaoh's right-hand.

GENESIS 38: 8–10

Said Judah to Onan, *'Your duty*
Is clearly to father a beauty!'
His nerve failed him when
He pulled out, there and then,
And died in the act! Naughty, naughty!

GENESIS 38: 12–30

Her father-in-law, namely Judah
Produced twins for Tamar. What cruder!
Red thread on his wrist
Zerah should be born first,
But Perez emerged as the leader!

GENESIS 39: 1–20

More intrigue. Wife of Potiphar
Seduced Jo – a steamy affair!
Producing his clothes
She said, '*Evidence shows*
He's the culprit! So jail him! Ha ha!'

GENESIS 39: 21–23

In prison did Joseph so well,
Promoted him fast, so they tell.
Intrigues nearly sunk him.
No one could debunk him
With God on his side, they just fell!

GENESIS 40

The butler and baker fell foul
Of Pharaoh. But then, wise old owl –
At Joseph's entreating
The butler kept meeting.
The baker he hanged! Let's all howl!

GENESIS 41

Pharaoh kept dreaming. *'What's this?'*
So Joseph interpreted. *'Gi'ss*
A mo to make plans
And store wheat in our barns –
And we'll give the famine a miss!'

GENESIS 42

His plans were so obviously neat
That people begged Egypt, to eat!
'Don't starve our poor nation
But give us salvation!'
His family, soon, Jo would meet.

GENESIS 43

Now Joseph soon saw who they were.
They still didn't know him. '*Please Sir,*'
They said, as he spoke
'*You're a very nice bloke!*'
But a test was on hand to make sure.

GENESIS 44

In Benjamin's sack, was a cup
That Joseph had hidden – straight up!
They found it too late
As they journeyed till eight –
He'd have to be hostage – the pup!

GENESIS 45: 4

But Joseph's pretence could not last.
'*I'm Joseph!*' he owned up. '*I've passed
Many years here at court
And you – all of you – thought
I had died in that pit you me cast.*'

GENESIS 45: 16–28

Pharaoh and Joseph were glad
And so was his family. *'The lad
Has done himself proud
So now we're all allowed
To tell the good news to our dad!'*

GENESIS 46: 1–7

So Israel determined, *'I'll see
What my sons reported to me!'*
To Egypt he moved
With the family he loved –
No happier dad there could be!

GENESIS 49

Disputes followed blessings galore
And finally, Israel was sure.
He took his last breath
As he went to his death –
His family at peace to the core.

EXODUS 1: 1–14

When Joseph had died, things got worse –
The Pharaoh decided to curse
All the Israelite folk
There in Egypt – no joke!
And got them brick making! So terse!

EXODUS 1: 15

The midwives were named – Shiphrah, Puah,
It seems there were only the two – er –
In all Israel!
They worked flat out! Well, well!
What else could two midwives do? Coo, er!

EXODUS 1: 16–22

He ordered the midwives to kill
All Israelite boys born, but still
To let the girls be.
But the orders, you see
Were all disobeyed, if you will!

Exodus 2: 1–4

A Levite girl after a while
Had baby son. Then by the Nile
She set him afloat
In a bullrush-made boat
For his future in Egypt in style!

Exodus 2: 5–10

The Pharaoh's young daughter passed by.
'Whatever is this, I espy?'
She picked up the boy,
Cuddled him like a toy
And named him her Moses. My, my!

Exodus 2: 11–15

When Moses grew up, he inspected
Some injustice, never expected.
An Egyptian bully
He slew, wholly, fully!
To Midian fled undetected.

EXODUS 2: 21

He lay low until one fine day
A beautiful girl came his way.
'Oh Zipporah, *dear*
Be my wife! Yes, right here!'
They married without more delay!

EXODUS 2: 22

Before long, a young son she bore
Called Gershom, *'The Israelite for*
A *stranger,'* he said
'In a strange land, I'm led!'
And Zippy and Moses said, 'Cor!'

EXODUS 3: 1–6

Now Moses was tending the sheep
One day when his conscience went *'Bleep!'*
'I'm God!' said the voice
'And you now have the choice –
The God of your fathers to keep!'

While tending his sheep, Moses saw
A huge bush on fire. *'What's the score?'*
He thought, as a voice
Called to him, 'Moses!' (twice)
'Right here!' – Moses said – *'Yes! What for?'*

The Lord said, 'Stay there! Don't get near!
Barefoot where you stand, you'll revere!'
On holy ground trod
Moses. *'I am the God*
Of Abe, Ike and Jake – is that clear?'

EXODUS 3: 6–12

'I am the God of your crowd –
Of Abraham, Isaac – I vowed –
And Jacob as well,
And I want you to tell
Every Israelite here. Now! Aloud!'

EXODUS 3: 12–14

'I've heard your prayer here from on high,
And I want you to know I'm nearby!'
'So what is Your name?'
Moses asked, heart aflame:
'I AM who I AM! It's no lie!'

EXODUS 3: 17–22

'My plan is to set you all free
From Egypt, and soon you will see
If you follow my word
To the letter you heard
From I AM who I AM – that's me!'

EXODUS 4: 1–5

'So how will they know that it's true?'
Asked Moses, of God. 'Well – when you
Strike hard with your rod –
As a snake from the sod
It will be!' 'Beat that!' Moses said – 'Phew!'

EXODUS 4: 6–7

If that wasn't funny enough,
The next trick would call Moses' bluff.
His hand, like a leper –
Looked something like pepper!
But then, back to normal! Just rough!

EXODUS 4: 8–16

'It's my way to tell you the truth'
Said God, 'You're no longer a youth!
So do as I say
And I'll show you the way
And no one will say you're uncouth!'

EXODUS 5: 1–3

So Moses kept on at Pharaoh
And nagged him, 'Release people, so!
We'll only be gone
For a feast.' (It's a con!)
'And over the Red Sea we'll go!'

EXODUS 5: 4-8

But Pharaoh increased their hard task.
'It's no good you coming to ask
To travel abroad
Just to worship your Lord! –
So wipe off the grin from your mask!'

EXODUS 5: 9-23

'Try making the bricks without straw!'
Said Pharaoh! 'And make plenty more!'
The Israelites worked
Hard, and nobody shirked,
But they yearned to show Moses the door!

EXODUS 6: 2-3

God said, 'Moses, this is My name
So holy, but don't take the blame!
It sounds like wind blowing.
YAHWEH gets you going!
The patriarchs called Me the same!'

EXODUS 6: 5–6

To Moses, God said, 'This is it!
And now you will see bit by bit
What power I possess!
So obey Me, unless
In slavery you want to sit!'

EXODUS 7: 8–13

So Moses and Aaron did tricks
To impress the Pharaoh, and fix
Their exodus out
Of Egypt, no doubt!
Then God planned a nastier mix!

EXODUS 7: 13–25

The first plague turned river to blood.
No water to drink. 'If we could
Just leave for three days?
'You stay put!' Pharaoh says,
But Moses continued to brood.

EXODUS 8: 1–15

'Just see how you like plagues of frogs!'
Said Moses to Pharaoh. 'It jogs
My memory here
That you might disappear!
Oh no – you stay put! Dirty dogs!'

EXODUS 8: 16–19

The next plague to come was the lice.
Pharaoh said, 'Moses – that's not nice!'
His magic men said
'Our spells kill all lice dead!'
But they didn't. And then came the flies!

EXODUS 8: 20–32

The flies plagued old Pharaoh right cruel.
'What is Moses up to, the fool?'
'Just let us go free
We'll come back, just you see!'
Said Moses, to Pharaoh, in duel.

EXODUS 9: 1–8

Despite Moses' efforts to rattle
Old Pharaoh, it still left the cattle.
'Watch me!' Moses said
As he nodded his head –
'This plague is far worse than a battle!'

EXODUS 9: 9–12

Each time Pharaoh changed his mind, he
Refused Moses' Israelites' plea.
So just for his toils
Pharaoh came out in boils
And that stung his pride, don't you see!

EXODUS 9: 13–35

He still wouldn't let Moses go,
So hail, fire and thunder, and snow
Was what God sent next –
As you read in the text.
But Pharaoh said 'No! – No! No! No!'

EXODUS 10: 1–20

'How about locusts, instead?'
Said Moses to Pharaoh. 'You said
That we could go free
But these plagues came, you see –
Because you would rather us dead!'

EXODUS 10: 21–29

'I tell you what,' Moses said then
'We'll blot out daylight! Come on, men!'
With Pharaoh enveloped,
The darkness developed!
'When will this all end, Moses, when?'

EXODUS 11

The time came for Moses to act.
Old Pharaoh had broken his pact.
'At midnight, yes we
Will be crossing the Sea!'
Moses said. Pharaoh laughed. Then he cracked!

Exodus 12: 1–28

'Instruct everybody,' Mo said
'And get everyone out of bed.
'Have roast lamb before,
And paint blood on the door,
So God's angel will pass overhead!'

Exodus 12: 29–51

The doorposts without any mark
Were earmarked for slaughter in dark.
But those who survived
By the Sea had arrived,
Awaiting instructions in park.

Exodus 13: 21–22

To navigate well, Moses saw
A pillar of fire by night, or
A cloud in the day
To help them make their way
From Egypt to Canaan, and more!

EXODUS 14: 15–21

The people were all at a loss.
'*However shall we get across?*'
But then – hand on heart –
Moses waved Sea apart,
And cried, '*God Almighty! You're Boss!*'

EXODUS 14: 22–26

The people crossed over in glee
On dry land, in midst of the Sea.
But Pharaoh raged on
With the Israelites gone –
'*Get them back!*' ordered Pharaoh, '*To me!*'

EXODUS 14: 27

His chariots came hard on their heel,
But mud just stuck fast to the wheel.
'*I think we are doomed!*'
Said Egyptians, entombed.
They drowned in the Sea. No big deal!

EXODUS 15: 1–18

Then Moses sang praise to the Lord:
'I thank You for keeping Your word!'
The women with timbrels
Sang, danced, to their cymbals
'We're free from old Pharaoh! Thank God!'

EXODUS 15: 19–21

The prophetess, Miriam, she
Danced, and shook her timbrel in glee!
'The Lord, He's been good
Because He understood
That Israel from Egypt should flee!'

EXODUS 15: 22–24

The trouble about such a journey
Showed Moses the need for attorney.
'The desert's so dry
If we don't drink, we'll die!'
The people complained, *'We'll go loony!'*

EXODUS 15: 25–27

The waters of Marah were banned,
But God had the matter in hand,
As Moses threw tree
Into water. 'Yippee! –
We can drink all we like, hand in hand!'

EXODUS 16: 1–13

Then came the grave matter of hunger
'We really can't go any longer!'
'Let no one complain!'
Just then, quails came like rain
As Moses dispatched a scaremonger.

EXODUS 16: 14–36

Next morning, when Moses arose
The ground there was covered like snows.
'Here's manna to eat!'
Moses said, *'It's a treat!*
Like wafers and honey it goes!'

EXODUS 17: 1–7

Then up came a serious complaint:
'If we don't get water – we'll faint!'
So using his rod
Moses struck rock. 'Oh God
Please help us!' 'You thirsty? – I ain't!'

EXODUS 17: 8–16

But battles ahead came too soon.
And Moses was weary at noon.
'We'll prop up his hand,
So they all understand
That Israel will win, and not swoon!'

EXODUS 19: 1–5

In Sinai, Moses' call came
From God, up the mountain – the same.
'Just keep all my laws
And my love will not pause.
You'll always be precious, by name!'

EXODUS 19: 6

'To me, you're a kingdom of priests
A nation that's holy. Like yeasts
Work wonders in flour,
All must come clean, this hour!' –
God spoke like an MC at feasts!

EXODUS 20: 1–11

'These are the laws you must keep:
Put God first. And images heap
In a pile. But God's name
You must never defame.
And take a day off for a sleep!'

EXODUS 20:12–16

'Give honour to mum and to dad,
And don't murder folk, 'cos that's bad!
Adultery's wrong
So is stealing, along
With saying your neighbour's a cad!'

EXODUS 20: 17–21

'You have all you need in this life,
So don't covet things that are rife –
Not animals, spouse,
Or possessions, or house!
Evil habits cut down with a knife!'

EXODUS 20: 22–26

'So long as we know where we stand,'
Said God, as he took Moses' hand,
'We'll get along fine –
Israelites, yours and mine!
My blessings will shower on the land!'

EXODUS 21

'My rules are quite simple, you see
We'll get on for ever, if we
Keep what we've agreed.
Then I promise your seed
Will flourish as sand by the sea!'

EXODUS 22–23

'In my ways, all folk should behave,
From birthday-time, right to the grave.
On festival days
Give me praise upon praise,
And value commandments I gave.'

EXODUS 24

'There's one thing more for you to do
At sacrifice time, I want you
To sprinkle the blood
On the people, like mud
Baths – as Covenant-trust we renew!'

EXODUS 25–28

'The next job for you is to make
The Ark of the Covenant. Take
The best things there are
From nearby and afar –
It must be superb, for My sake!'

EXODUS 29

'The Ark's guardians must be appointed!
With holy oil, now be anointed.
The priests will then bear
Their God's Ark everywhere,
So Israel will not be disjointed.'

EXODUS 32: 1–6

Aaron, meanwhile, had a thought
Of jazzing-up Israel with sport.
A calf made of gold
Would be fine to behold!
But would it be right? Did he ought?

EXODUS 32: 7–14

Then Moses was fiercely enraged
With wickedness Aaron had staged.
He called folk together
To question them whether
On God's side their names should be paged?

EXODUS 32: 19–35

Their dancing around golden calf
Made Moses say, 'I'll break in half
The tablets of stone!
Let no Israelite moan!'
He banged on the ground with his staff!

EXODUS 33: 1–16

'Sooner or later,' God said
'You'll have your own land, and be fed
With milk and with honey
It's really quite funny!
Ex-Egypt, forty years, instead!'

EXODUS 33: 17–23

'Show me Your glory, I pray'
Said Moses to God, late one day.
'You can't glimpse My face,
But My back part will race
Past you, Moses. Ready? Then stay!'

EXODUS 34: 1–28

Next morning, up Sinai marched
Old Moses, his lips pretty parched!
'I'll write them again!'
Said God, 'You take the strain!
Commandments, Mark 2, ironed and starched!'

EXODUS 34: 29 – 35: 35

His face shone, as if well sun-burned
From seeing God. Moses returned
And started again
All the people to train
In God's ways – the ones he had learned.

EXODUS 36–40

The Covenant-Ark needed men
All well-trained and loyal, so then
The rituals seen
Were well-done, smart and clean –
Understood in the Israelites' den.

LEVITICUS

The third book of Moses spells out
What Israel's religion's about.
The rules were so clear
No law-keeper need fear,
And it organised all without doubt!

The priests' job was keeping all sure
The nation was constantly pure.
What God had in mind
Was so well underlined,
There was nothing the priests could not cure!

NUMBERS

In Numbers, recorded as stated
The Twelve Tribes of Israel rated
Their weakness and strength,
And their territory's length
For posterity – even though dated!

NUMBERS 1: 1–2

At the meeting tent, soldiers fell in!
You couldn't be heard for the din –
But Moses spoke loudly
And so very proudly –
He hoped they would take it all in!

NUMBERS 1: 1–46

Men twenty years old, who could fight,
Were numbered as warriors. Right!
Six hundred and three
Thousand five fifty. '*We*
Shall guard Israel's camp day and night!'

NUMBERS 6: 1–21

The vow of a Nazirite meant
That hair should be long. The intent
Of not drinking wine
Or lush grapes from the vine
Was to keep him God's special servant.

NUMBERS 6: 24–26

'The Lord bless you, Israel, and keep you!
The Lord make His face to shine on you!
The Lord lift up His
Countenance on you! This
Will give you His peace. Israel, it's true!'

NUMBERS 8: 23–26

Levites, at fifty, retire.
Their priestly work has to expire.
But ministering still
For their God, yes, it will
Be spiritually part of their fire.

NUMBERS 10: 1–10

The priests, who were all Aaron's sons
Blew trumpet sounds, signalling ones
Which sounded alarm,
Or just gave Israel calm.
At festivals, they blew great guns!

NUMBERS 10: 33–36

Wherever they travelled, in front
The Ark of the Covenant went.
It was covered by cloud
And no man was allowed
To touch it, unless it was meant.

NUMBERS 11: 1–9

'We reckon that Egypt was good
With free fish, and cucumbers! Food
Such as garlic and leeks
Which we ain't had for weeks!
And melons – not manna for pud!'

NUMBERS 11: 10–22

So God sent them quails as they'd asked
It was easy for God, multitasked!
'For a month at the first
Eat them up till you burst –
Till quails through your noses have passed!'

NUMBERS 12: 31–35

Such food made the people go crazy
In an orgy of lust, things went hazy.
A lot of them died
When God's word was defied –
So they buried them under the daisy!

NUMBERS 12: 1–3

To Moses, the meekest of men,
God suddenly spoke there and then:
'You, only, *have seen*
Where my presence has been.
But for others, just visions, I ken!'

NUMBERS 13

From each tribe of Israel, a guy
Was sent out by Moses, to spy
Out Canaan's land
Which God promised to hand
To them one day! God doesn't lie!

NUMBERS 14

The chaps started grumbling a lot:
'We had better times – (than we've got
Now) – in Egypt, as slaves!
Let's go back through the waves!'
But Moses and Aaron said, 'Not!'

NUMBERS 16

Ringleaders, Dathan, Abiram,
Were scolded by Moses. 'Let's fire 'em!'
At which came a quake
That devoured them! 'We'll make
Them sorry the people once hired 'em!'

NUMBERS 17

Up his sleeve Moses had one more trick.
Each tribe had to plant its own stick
In the ground. It would grow
If God wanted it so.
And Levi's one blossomed right quick!

NUMBERS 18: 21–24

'Give God ten per cent as your due,'
Said Moses, 'And then it will do
As payment for work
By the Levites. Don't lurk
Near the Meeting Tent curtains – yes, you!'

NUMBERS 19

He issued lots more regulations
For hygiene, and healthy relations.
'Make sure you keep clean!
Wash your hands when you've been!'
And that's how they maintained their stations.

NUMBERS 21: 4–9

The people, all bitten by snakes,
Said sorry. 'Just do what it takes!' –
They begged. Moses made
A brass snake, and he laid
It on a big pole. 'Ditch the fakes!'

NUMBERS 22

As Balaam rode his faithful ass,
'I'll face these guys at mountain pass!'
'I'm stopping right now!'
Said the ass, 'and here's how!'
So Balaam reversed pretty fast!

NUMBERS 25

In order to keep the tribes pure
Rough justice prevailed, to be sure.
Phineas's spear
Killed a man and his dear –
Just that – an expedient cure!

NUMBERS 26

A roll-call was taken that day
And six hundred thousand said 'Yea!'
'The land you will take
By proportion. You'll make
A nation for me,' God said. 'Aye!'

NUMBERS 27

'Choose somebody spiritual, one
Like Joshua, the son of Nun.
It's he who will lead us
And equally need us!
Together, the battles are won!'

NUMBERS 28–31

God gave Moses more rules again
The Israelites learned them with pain.
'If you want to succeed
Then obey them, indeed!'
Said Moses, 'Then Canaan we'll gain!'

NUMBERS 32

This side of the Jordan, the land
Was good enough, and in their hand.
Said Moses, 'We oughta
Cross o'er Jordan's water! —
Just so you all know where you stand!'

NUMBERS 33

Despite some of their tittle-tattle
The Israelites focussed on battle.
'It's ours for the taking!'
Cried Moses, awaking
'So let's herd them up just like cattle!'

DEUTERONOMY 1

In Deuteronomy we see
Encouragement, for all to be
True, to God the Lord,
And to give God their word –
From now and to eternity.

DEUTERONOMY 2

The military campaign began,
And orders were sent to each clan
To pass by in peace
Or to battle, then cease.
'Our goal is to conquer Canaan!'

DEUTERONOMY 4

Moses strove hard to exhort
The strong men of Israel who fought
With an eye on their sword
And an eye on God's word,
For this way the victory's bought!

DEUTERONOMY 5

The Lord made His Covenant stand.
All people here should understand
'His commandments – all ten
Should be learned and done! Then
God's blessings will rest in our hand.'

DEUTERONOMY 6

'O Israel, hear this,' Moses cried,
'Our God is one God. We have tried
To love God – that's right,
With heart, soul, and with might!
So no one can say that we've lied!'

DEUTERONOMY 7

'Wherever you come across falsehood
In worship, these idols are no good!
So break them all down
Never mind if they frown!
Just worship the one God as you should!'

DEUTERONOMY 8

'But when you become pretty rich
Don't take all the credit, but ditch
Your pride in the bin!
It was God helped you win
Your wealth, and your health, without hitch!'

DEUTERONOMY 10: 12

'What God requires of you all here:
Just follow His ways, and revere
Him, with heart and soul.
Give Him all – yes the whole
Of your love and devotion. That clear?'

DEUTERONOMY 12–26

The next fourteen chapters are law,
To know right from wrong as before.
For instance, 'Don't eat
Certain species of meat,
Or you'll bring Israel's reign to the floor!'

DEUTERONOMY 15

'Make sure that you look after all
Who on bad times so harshly fall –
The poor and the weak,
And those who can't speak
For themselves, whether they're short or tall!'

DEUTERONOMY 17

'Justice must always be done
And seen to work fairly. It's fun
When all play the game.
Keep the rules, and God's Name
Will go round the world, Number One!'

DEUTERONOMY 21

'A man who has sinned really badly
Will hang on a tree, rather sadly.
But take him down, men,
Before sunset – and then
Get him buried. With that done – go gladly!'

DEUTERONOMY 26

'At harvest-time, make sure your best
Is given to God. It's a test
To judge your devotion.
So set things in motion
Right now, while your life has some zest!'

DEUTERONOMY 27

This chapter is all about curses,
For folk – who do wrong – lie in hearses!
'Just make sure that you
Do what God wants you to –
And then you won't need the wet-nurses!'

DEUTERONOMY 30

'So yet again comes the reminder
To keep faith with God. He'll be kinder
If you keep your word
And be true to your Lord –
This pact is a man-and-God binder!'

DEUTERONOMY 32

Here Moses breaks out into song.
He has to – for he hasn't long!
He finally dies
In a grave the right size.
Don't know where! If you do, then you're wrong!

JOSHUA 1

The Lord said to Joshua, 'Rise,
And with Moses dead, just be wise!
Be strong as you go,
Cross the Jordan's full flow!
And spy out Canaan for size!'

JOSHUA 2: 1–14

Young Rahab lived by the town wall
At Jericho. Before nightfall
Came two Jewish spies.
'Shield us! Nobody dies
Here! Know our protection's for all!'

JOSHUA 2: 15–24

Escape was not easy, but she –
With rope from her window, you see –
Let both spies get down
Out of Jericho town.
They, true to their word, let her be!

JOSHUA 3

Said Joshua, *'Follow the Ark,*
At Jordan's banks you'll need to park.'
No sooner arrived
There, the waters contrived
To allow them to cross before dark!

JOSHUA 5

Once over the Jordan, they go
In battle to win Jericho.
But God said, *'Your feet*
Must be bare, as is meet
When standing on holy ground!' So!

JOSHUA 6: 1–19

The priests with their trumpets and Ark
Round Jericho's walls sounded. *'Hark!'*
Said all the town people
When walls rocked, as steeple
In gales. Dogs then started to bark!

JOSHUA 6: 20

They marched seven days round the walls,
And cheered, and blew their trumpet-calls!
The people went hoarse
With their shouting, of course,
Till Bang! Crash! All Jericho falls!

JOSHUA 7

Some looting took place in the city
Of Ai, and it was a pity.
'It's just got to stop!'
Joshua said, *'And I'll cop*
All looters with death – stoned, and gritty!'

JOSHUA 10

The battles raged on, and they won,
As Joshua looked up at the sun
And moon. They stood still.
But the battle raged till
The Israelites' warfare was done.

JOSHUA 14: 6–15

At eighty-five, Caleb said *'I*
Am strong as I ever was. My
Inheritance, Hebron,
Was Moses' gift – and on
My God I will always rely!'

JOSHUA 24: 17

The conquest of Canaan progressed
As Israelite soldiers confessed
That what they'd achieved
Was because they believed
In God. Their pact – put to the test!

JUDGES 1

With Joshua dead, Israel sought
To elect a strong leader who fought
With God on his side –
Only enemies died,
With Israelite casualties nought!

JUDGES 4: 17–24

Jael, the same – Heber's wife
Decided against use of knife.
With tent-peg in head
She killed Sisera dead!
So ended a chapter of strife!

JUDGES 5

Deborah sang praise, for God
Delivered them all on the nod!
She summed up the war
In a few lines or more,
Starting forty years' peace on their tod!

JUDGES 7: 1–4

This is where Gideon came in.
The odds were against him. *'Begin*
To choose some sound men
Who are trustworthy, then
I'll lead you,' said God, *'and you'll win!'*

JUDGES 7: 5–7

Some lay down their weapons to lap
The water up. It was a trap!
But, weapons kept ready,
Some drank, cupped hands steady –
Three hundred best soldiers on tap!

JUDGES 7: 8–18

Each vessel concealed a lit torch,
And Gideon ordered them, '*March!*
When the trumpet I blow —
Break the vessels, and so
Wreak surprise on the enemy's patch!'

JUDGES 7: 19–25

'The sword of the Lord!' they all cried
'Of Gideon, too!' — Foe defied!
Their trumpets they blew!
Such a hullabaloo!
And God spread their victory wide!

JUDGES 8: 33–35

No sooner had Gideon died
When Israel denounced God, and cried
'*We want orgies now*
Long live Baal! That's how
We want to enjoy life inside!'

JUDGES 9: 50–53

Abimelech approached a tower
'*I'll burn it down within the hour!*'
As these words he said
A millstone hit his head,
And pretty well killed him. Poor flower!

JUDGES 9: 54–55

He didn't want people to know
A woman had beaten him. So
He begged to be slain
By his own sword. The pain
Was less than the shame of her blow!

JUDGES 11

Filled with the Spirit, he vowed
'*I, Jephthah, do say this aloud:*
If God's on my side
Then we all shall abide
In peace!' And to God's law he bowed!

JUDGES 12: 6

One way they kept some things in check
Was how to pronounce 'Sh.' Oh heck!
Not '*Sibboleth*' pure,
But it's '*Shibboleth!*' – sure –
The password all phonies would wreck!

JUDGES 14: 5–6

Here, Samson comes onto the scene
The Spirit of God in him. Keen
To show off his strength
A young lion, full length
He conquered. '*It's nothing, I mean!*'

JUDGES 14: 7–9

So Samson walked back at his ease,
And came across hundreds of bees!
Inside lion's body
They swarmed, and yet oddly
From strong came forth sweetness! Yes, please!

JUDGES 15: 3–5

Samson wreaked havoc one night –
Caught three hundred foxes. Alight
He turned them into
Philistines' wheatfield too!
And gave all a jolly great fright!

JUDGES 15: 9–15

The Philistines camped near a pass
Where Samson met them, but alas –
He killed them, killed all
Quite a thousand men fall
By his weapon: a jawbone of ass!

JUDGES 16: 6

Delilah tried using her charm
This Samson chap's strong in the arm!
'*How are you so strong
Big chap? Now, come along –
I promise to do you no harm!*'

JUDGES 16: 8-9

The Philistines tested Sam out.
With ropes, they secured him up. 'Lout!'
They jeered at him. Then
He burst free, yet again!
His strength was legendary, no doubt!

JUDGES 16: 11-12

'OK!' Sam said, 'Tie me up tight
And I'll be your slave every night!'
But this was a tease –
She was weak at the knees
When Samson broke loose! What a sight!

JUDGES 16: 13-14

'Just tie me up tight by my hair,'
Said Samson. 'Is that pretty fair?'
Delilah stood back
When the ropes snapped. Bang! Crack!
'You'll not find my weakness. So there!'

JUDGES 16: 21–29

When, shaved by Delilah, Sam's cries –
As the Philistines gouged out his eyes –
Came as he pushed hard
On the pillars, like lard
In his hands, they gave way. Some surprise!

JUDGES 16: 30–31

Three thousand had come for some sport
To see Samson's strength. But he caught
Them all, as he died –
See the pillars collide!
He slew more in death than he fought!

RUTH 1

Our Ruth was a Moabitess,
At Bethlehem, her new address.
She went out to glean
In the wheatfields. *'I've seen
The man to be mine, if God bless!'*

Ruth 2

'To *Boaz, I want to be wed,*'
Said Ruth, hoping he would be led
In her sure direction.
With eagle detection
Invited her, '*Glean here!*' he said.

Ruth 3

She snuggled up with him that night
And he was not certain it's right.
But later next day
He did pay his way –
His troth, Boaz to Ruth did plight!

Ruth 4

It means that the family tree
Of David, through Jesse, will be.
Jesse's father – oh joy! –
Came through Ruth's baby boy!
The Jews' royal line, don't you see!

1 SAMUEL 1

Elkanah and Hannah – though old
Produced baby Samuel, we're told.
He was *'Asked of the Lord.'*
And they went overboard
With excitement, increasing their fold!

1 SAMUEL 2: 1–21

In song Hannah burst out! – His birth
For her – was like no one's on earth!
So precious was he.
'In God's service he'll be!'
And as Eli's mate, caused him mirth.

1 SAMUEL 2: 22–26

Now Eli was well on in years
When rumours came into his ears.
'Your sons, we have found,
With the girls sleep around!' –
And so increased Eli's worst fears!

1 SAMUEL 3: 1–5

Eli was once sound asleep
When Samuel heard his name bleep.
'You called me?' Sam said
'What! Asleep in my bed?
Just go back and keep counting sheep!'

1 SAMUEL 3: 6–21

'I'm here, Lord!' – Sam said it again.
So Eli said, 'Keep saying then:
'Speak Lord, for I'm here!
I'm Your servant!' – and hear
What the Lord has to say. It's so plain!'

1 SAMUEL 4

The Philistines captured the prize –
The Israelite Ark. They told wise
Old Eli, but he
Being ninety-eight, see –
Of shock died in front of their eyes.

1 SAMUEL 5–6

In those seven months such harm fell
On Philistines, Dagon, as well!
They sent it back nice
With gold tumours, gold mice,
With jewels and gold! Ain't that swell!

1 SAMUEL 7

In Kiriath-Jearim, it stood
For twenty years, just as it should.
At Mizpah, Sam prayed
That all Israel had made
A promise to turn to God. Good!

1 SAMUEL 8

The people nagged Sam day and night
'We want a king! We think it's right!'
But Samuel warned
That the day hadn't dawned –
But he'd put it to God – yes, that night!

1 SAMUEL 9–10

God answered Sam's prayer pretty fast
For Saul arrived. *'He's here at last!'*
Anointed with oil
Saul became king and all –
The Lord's will on him had been cast!

1 SAMUEL 10

He called all the tribes to meet there
'You wanted a king! – Well, I'm here!'
The people went mad!
'He's the first king we've had!
God save him! God answered our prayer!'

1 SAMUEL 11: 14–15

Said Samuel, *'Come, let us go*
To Gilgal, and there we shall show
The world we renew
The kingdom! O'er you
Saul's king! We rejoice! Ain't that so!'

1 Samuel 14

This Jon, of King Saul, the young son
Succeeded in battle, and won.
But angered his dad
'He must die! Yes, my lad!'
The people's great hero – this one!

1 Samuel 16: 7

Quite clearly, a man's outward show
Is what people look at. But no!
It matters much more
What his heart is all for!
The Lord looks at that, don't you know!

1 Samuel 16: 4–13

At Bethlehem, David was found
When Samuel, family around
Anointed this lad.
'You'll be king!' That's not bad!
God's Spirit in him did abound!

1 SAMUEL 16: 21–23

Saul felt rather down in the dumps
God's anger with him was like mumps!
When David arrived,
Played his harp, Saul revived,
And no more experienced the humps!

1 SAMUEL 17: 1–37

The Philistines had a huge son –
Goliath, their bold champion.
He challenged Israel:
*'Will no one there avail
To fight me?'* Thus Gol thought he'd won!

1 SAMUEL 17: 38

Saul thought that he'd done the right thing
In kitting-out David. *'I'll bring
My armour for you
To wear.'* 'But it won't do' –
Said David, *'I'll just use my sling!'*

1 SAMUEL 17: 48–51

So David, the youngest of three
Accepted his challenge. And he
With sling aimed at forehead
Killed Goliath stone dead.
Beheaded him, for all to see!

1 SAMUEL 18

David and Jonathan, they were
Such friends, they were soul-mates! Yes, Sir!
But Saul wasn't pleased
When the womenfolk wheezed
'Young David's far braver than you are!'

1 SAMUEL 18: 10–12

Saul's envy had boiled over when
He vowed to kill David. But then
He lunged with his spear
Twice, and so very near,
But God shielded David. Amen!

1 Samuel 18: 20–30

Saul set this young David a task
'One hundred Phili-skins, I ask –
And then you may marry
My daughter. Don't tarry!'
Dave scissored two hundred in cask!

1 Samuel 19

They patched up bad feeling, but Saul
Tried hard to spear Dave in the hall.
He missed David's ear,
But Michal got to hear.
Dave fled through her window, down wall.

1 Samuel 21

Dave met the priest Ahimelech
Who said, *'Why alone? What the heck?*
Hey – don't eat that bread –
'Cos it's holy, I said!'
But Dave scoffed the lot without check!

1 SAMUEL 22: 1

So David escaped to a cave
The one of Adullam, and gave
Four hundred men
Good advice, there and then,
And became their leader. How brave!

1 SAMUEL 25

Dave wedded this young Abigail,
Companion wife to young Michal,
Ahinoam, she
Became wife number three –
No wonder Dave looked rather pale!

1 SAMUEL 28

At Shunem, the Philistines' pitch
Was too close for Saul. Then a witch
At Endor foresaw
That Saul's life was no more!
'Tomorrow, you'll die in the ditch!'

1 Samuel 31

Saul's fortunes, this time, all turned sour
'The witch told me it's my last hour!'
He suicide faced,
Just to die undisgraced.
The Philistines' victory brought power!

2 Samuel 1

Dave heard about Saul's death, as well
As Jonathan's, whom he loved well.
He sang a lament
For his friend who had meant
Such love in his life – it was hell!

2 Samuel 3: 31–36

At Abner's death, David was shocked.
Alliance with him had been rocked.
Yet the people approved
All Dave did, and they loved
Him, and to King David they flocked!

2 SAMUEL 5: 1–10

So David was now truly king.
All Israel, his subjects. '*I sing*
Jerusalem – thou
Art my home – and from now
The City of David's the thing!'

2 SAMUEL 6: 1–10

The Ark was the centre of dance
And music, a festival trance.
Poor Uzzah died there
As he touched it. Unfair –
For his oxen had stumbled just once!

2 SAMUEL 6: 11–19

For three months, the Ark rested still
At Obed-Edom's, yes, until
One day David said
That the Ark must instead
Be housed on Jerusalem's hill!

2 SAMUEL 9

He – Mephibosheth – was the son
Of Jonathan, he was the one
Whom David invited
So very excited –
But lame in both feet. Not much fun!

2 SAMUEL 10

Dave showed Hanun some deep contrition
Sent servants on a nice peace mission.
But they greatly feared
When he shaved half their beard,
Cut clothes in two. What a condition!

2 SAMUEL 11

Now David had earmarked a beauty,
Bath-sheba was his cutie cutie!
He fixed it so plain
That Uriah was slain –
Her husband. She's now David's booty!

2 SAMUEL 12: 1–14

Nathan met David one day,
Told-off in no uncertain way!
'This baby will die
But you really must try
To behave as God wants you. OK!'

2 SAMUEL 12: 24–31

So sorry was Dave, but contrite
He comforted Bath-sheba. 'Might
We try once again?
Shall we name him. Like when?'
'Er – Solomon sounds about right!'

2 SAMUEL 13: 1–33

David's son, Amnon, tricked Tamar
His sister. He – bad evil schemer –
Seduced her to bed,
But got slain. So it's said –
Their father put out a disclaimer!

2 SAMUEL 13: 34–38

Absalom – he was their dad –
Just ran off with all he had.
King David was grieving
At both his sons leaving.
Small comfort, now Amnon was dead!

2 SAMUEL 18

The crunch came when Absalom strove
To fight dad in battle. He drove
Right into an oak,
But got hanged! His last croak –
While his mule carried on up the grove.

2 SAMUEL 21: 15–22

Four Philistine soldiers, at Gath –
Six fingers, six toes one man hath –
Like giants, so tall
Each one slain, died. Thus all
Of Israel could get back its breath!

2 SAMUEL 22

Old David waxed lyrical too –
And praised God for everything. 'You
Delivered us all –
Saved Israel! I call
All people to join me. Thank You!'

2 SAMUEL 23–24

These were David's last words in verse,
When things there went from bad to worse.
A pestilence great
Plagued the people – but wait!
He paid for the peace through his purse!

1 KINGS 1: 1–4

The days came, as David got old
His body felt more of the cold.
A girl, Abishag
Warmed him. He said, '*I sag!* –
I realise I'm losing my hold!'

1 KINGS 1: 28—31

David called Bathsheba near –
'I'm naming your son king, my dear!'
He said, 'Go tell Zadok
And Nathan, the old crock –
That Solomon's next in line here!'

1 KINGS 1: 32—40

So Solomon saddled his mule
And came to them. 'Son – you're God's tool!'
Said David. 'You're king
From now on – please sing!'
Anointed by Zadok. That's cool!

1 KINGS 2: 1—11

So David instructed his son
In all regal things that were done.
And when David died
He was buried inside
Jerusalem's city. Grave One.

1 Kings 2: 12–25

Adonijah, Sol's young bro
Asked Bathsheba: 'Mummy, *please go*
And beg him to bless
As my wife, Abi-S!'
But Sol said, 'No! Kill him! *The foe!'*

1 Kings 3: 1–14

Solomon said in a dream
'*I'm nothing like David!'* A gleam
Came into his eye
When God said, '*By and by*
You'll be strong, rich and wise. Stay abeam!'

1 Kings 3: 16–22

Two mums each had babies all right,
But one baby died in the night.
The first mum infers
That the live one is hers,
So the other mum started a fight!

1 KINGS 3: 23–25

These mums tested Solomon's wares
They each claimed the baby was theirs.
'Then cut him in two!'
King Sol said, 'And then you
Will know who's the true mum! Who dares!'

1 KINGS 3: 26–28

At that stage, the real mum cried out –
'Don't kill my son!' – she had to shout
To make King Sol see
And realise it was she
Who was the true mum, without doubt!

1 KINGS 4

God blessed him with wisdom so wise
That Solomon's fame reached the skies –
His proverbs and songs –
Almost endless! In throngs
People came there to see him – a prize!

1 KINGS 5–7

The first thing Sol said they would do
To honour God, 'We'll build Jeru-
Salem the finest
Temple! – Yes, we build best!
The world will come here for the view!'

1 KINGS 8: 12–21

They then brought the Ark up as well.
It had its own place, it was swell!
The tablets of stone
Moses brought down alone
Inside it. Such glory – priests fell!

1 KINGS 8: 22–30

Solomon with all his might
Prayed hard to God. 'In Your sight
Let this temple be
Holy always, for thee
And we'll praise You here, day and night!'

1 KINGS 8: 54–66

The temple now built, Sol spoke loud
'All Israel will praise God, I vowed!
We'll have a great feast
Fourteen days at the least –
And we'll party till late, with a crowd!'

1 KINGS 10: 1–13

It's not every day you can say
'The Queen of Sheba came today!'
But Sol gave her all
Her desire – what a ball –
And answered her questions! Hooray!

1 KINGS 10: 14–29

King Sol spent a lot of his 'dough'
On cleaning the temple up, so
It really looked swell
And God liked it as well!
Such grand ideas! What a great show!

1 KINGS 11: 1–8

King Sol rather spread it around,
A thousand strange women he found.
Forgetting his vow
To the true God, he's now
All for pagan gods, stuck in the ground!

1 KINGS 11: 9–43

Rivalry threatened his reign –
Gave Solomon problems again.
It was over quite soon
But he died close on noon.
In Jerusalem's grave he was lain.

1 KINGS 12: 1–21

The kingdom divided in two.
'King Jereboam, we're with you!' –
Said those in the city
Jerusalem pretty –
For others Rehoboam would do!

1 KINGS 12: 28–33

Jerry did naughty things then –
Made two golden calves, and said 'Men,
You'll now worship these,
We can do as we please!'
At Bethel, and Dan, once again!

1 KINGS 13: 1–32

Came one day, from Judah a man
Who challenged his evil ways. 'Can
You be so disloyal
To God? Then the oil –
That anointed you king – never ran!'

This challenge made King Jerry think.
'It's true. I've done wrong! At the brink
Of things going awry
I'll repent 'ere I die!'
But meant it not. We saw him wink!

1 Kings 13: 33–34

In fact, Jerry sinned all the more,
His household, rotten to the core.
With drink and with feast
He anointed as priest
Whomever he came across. Cor!

1 Kings 14: 1–20

King Jerry persuaded his wife
To disguise herself, for the life
Of Abijah now
Was in peril, but wow!
Despite intrigue, son died. Such strife!

1 Kings 14: 21–31

Although Jerry's sinning was sad,
Rehoboam, his bro, was as bad!
In fact, it was worse
Far too bad for this verse –
And Reho was buried with dad!

1 Kings 15: 1–9

Abijam now wore the crown
And ruled in Jerusalem town.
But he soon died too –
It must surely be true –
As Asa the new king sat down.

1 Kings 15: 23 – 16: 34

Various kings reigned in turn
Each died, and was buried. We learn
That kings, bad or good,
In Jerusalem, should
Be judged for their deeds. Some would burn!

1 Kings 17

Elijah the Tishbite came by
And lodged with a widow nearby.
Her food kept on growing,
Her son healed. *'Worth knowing –
This prophet of God is some guy!'*

1 KINGS 18: 17–21

Elijah, now at Mount Carmel
Met prophets, the ones of Baal.
'A contest we'll set
To see whose God will get
These bonfires alight. Chaps – you'll fail!'

1 KINGS 18: 22–39

The Baal chaps tried hard all day
No fire from their gods came their way.
Despite drenched with water –
Alight El's one caught-a,
And Elijah's God won. Hooray!

1 KINGS 19

Elijah in cave refuge took
And faced wind and earthquake that shook
The ground round him there,
Also fire. *'Be aware'* –
'I'm God!' said a still small voice. *'Look!'*

1 KINGS 21

Jezebel played dirty tricks on
Poor Naboth. 'The blighter – I'll fix un!'
She said, and wrote lies
To her Ahab's surprise –
And Naboth was killed. What a vixen!

1 KINGS 22: 8

A faithful young prophet was he.
'Samaria, I say you'll see
God's wrath on all them
As in Jerusalem!'
Micaiah: Eighth century BC.

1 KINGS 22: 29–40

King Ahab was hit. Arrow's point
Sunk into him just where the joint
Of his armour was weak.
'With my last breath, I speak:
'My son Ahaziah anoint!'

2 KINGS 1

King A'ziah had drunk too much wine
And fell through the window – a sign
He'd lived his life wrong
In God's sight. Before long
He died – as Elijah said! Fine!

2 KINGS 2: 7–8

Elijah took his coat, and hit
The river Jordan, and then it
Divided in two
As the prophet passed through
And so did Elisha! That's it!

2 KINGS 2: 9–13

Elisha said, *'I'd like to see
Double your spirit on me!'*
Then a chariot of fire
Whisked Elijah much higher
To heaven. Yes – that's where he'll be!

2 Kings 2: 23–35

Elisha was off to Bethel.
When children there started to yell
'Hi, *baldy!*' they said –
Then two bears killed them dead –
All forty-two children! Well, well!

2 Kings 4

At Shunem, in her B & B,
Elisha asked, '*All this for me?* –
A *stool, table, bed,*
And a candlestick!' Said
Mine hostess, '*That's all you'll need, see!*'

2 Kings 5: 1–12

Leprous Naaman refused
To wash in the Jordan. Confused –
'*The Damascus rivers*
Just give me the shivers!
So what should I do?' Naaman mused.

2 KINGS 5: 13–14

'If one day I'd asked you to do
Some great deed, then come on – would you
Have done it?' 'Of course!'
Naaman ordered his horse.
In Jordan, seven dips cured him, too!

2 KINGS 6: 24–30

The famine had reached a high peak
When two mums agreed that this week
They'd both eat a son.
So next day they ate one –
But Mum 2 backed out, with a shriek!

2 KINGS 9

When King Jehu came to Jezreel,
She shouted abuse – Jezebel.
He said, 'Throw her down!'
Her blood splattered the town,
Bits and pieces were all they could feel!

2 KINGS 10: 1–28

King Jehu demolished the lot –
Supporters of Ahab. He got
Rid of Baal pagans –
Like meat is to vegans!
Thus Israel returned to God. What!

2 KINGS 10: 29–36

Kept Jehu – the calves made of gold
At Bethel and Dan, as of old.
He paid for it, though,
Shunning God, they say so –
For twenty-eight years, then – stone cold!

2 KINGS 11–16

The pattern for page after page
Is of kings doing things in their age
Like serving the Lord
Or not heeding His word –
Yet all achieved death as their wage!

2 KINGS 17

The king of Assyria came
And defamed the Israelites' name.
Deported, they grew
Even worse than they knew,
And God got fed up with them. Shame!

2 KINGS 22

With Josiah king, a change came.
He worshipped God, adored His name.
In a temple spring-clean –
'Look what I've found!' He'd seen
The Book of the Law. Very same!

2 KINGS 23: 1–2

So he read it from cover to cover
And said it again, and then over
Again. *'Yes, one knows
What the Covenant shows –
Let's do it, Israel, to recover!'*

2 Kings 23: 3–20

All pagan things Josiah heaved –
The idols, and cloth women weaved.
He dumped all the junk
Like a zealous young monk –
All purged for their good, he believed!

2 Kings 23: 21–28

King Josiah also restored
The Passover feast, much ignored
For dozens of years.
Unique king, it appears –
Unusually true to his Lord!

2 Kings 24

Nebuchadnezzar appeared
And deported Israel. They feared
They'd never return.
From Babylon. 'Burn
The temple down!' King Nebbie said!

1 CHRONICLES 1–8

It seemed like a good idea then
To list all the Israelite men
And women, q.v.
Israelite family tree,
In eight lengthy chapters. Amen!

1 CHRONICLES 9–29

This book summarises events
From the days Israel lived in tents
To King David's death,
Right up to his last breath.
Of history, tries to make sense.

2 CHRONICLES 1–36

This all starts with Solomon's reign
Repeats Israel's history again.
It ends with good news:
Persian King Cyrus' views:
'*Return to Jerus'lem's domain!*'

Ezra 1

Cyrus was stirred by the Lord
'*Return Israel's people!*' His word
He kept. Gave back freely
What Nebbie had really
Just stolen, and taken on board.

Ezra 3: 1–9

Once back in Jerusalem they
Began to put straight all affray.
The workmen strove hard
Day and night in the yard.
In two years, were well on their way.

Ezra 3: 10–13

A shout went up there on the day
When foundation stone – so they say
For the temple was laid
People wept – it relayed
So loud – they were heard miles away!

EZRA 6

Their enemies, sick to the core
Learned soon of the temple restore.
The whole thing exceeded
The size that was needed
When Solomon built his, before!

EZRA 10

A problem concerning those who
Had foreigners married. 'Hey, you
Must give up your wives
If you value your lives!
No more foreign wives, from hereto!'

NEHEMIAH 2: 1–9

Nehemiah was the one
Artaxerxes trusted. 'You, son
Must go back home now.
Build the walls up! And bow!'
Jerusalem's glory begun!

NEHEMIAH 2: 11–20

Neh spent three days scouring the city.
Such devastation! What a pity!
Encouraged, they vowed
To rebuild and be proud
Of their work. That's the whole nitty-gritty!

NEHEMIAH 4

Some people opposed what they did.
So it became urgent to rid
Themselves of the trouble.
They worked themselves double
With guards there, while the workers hid.

NEHEMIAH 5

There's always someone on the fiddle,
And Neh spotted this. '*It's a riddle*,'
He said, '*why you charge*
Extortionately large
Fees for your work! Restore it all!'

NEHEMIAH 7

A list was made up of those who
Returned to Jerusalem to
Begin all again
And forget all the pain
Of exile in Babylon. Phew!

NEHEMIAH 8

Ezra again read the law
In front of the people, before
They forgot all the ways
Of the Lord all their days! –
Those present bowed low to adore.

NEHEMIAH 9

The people agreed to take note
Of what they should do – learned by rote
The rituals they
Should observe day by day –
And no more put God to the vote!

NEHEMIAH 10

Reminded of what Moses said
Was what Israel's people heard read.
It made sense to all
To live up to God's call,
And that way, their path would be led.

NEHEMIAH 11

To live in the city, they cast
By lots, amongst them, and they passed
All these good ideas
As God's will for the years
Ahead. They blessed all, first and last.

NEHEMIAH 13

It still needed work to be done
To get all the people as one
To observe the law.
And for every small flaw
Neh cracked the whip. That bit was fun!

ESTHER 1: 1–11

Ahasuerus, yes, the king
Put on a great feast. Just the thing!
From India to
Ethiopia too
His empire extended. Ding ding!

ESTHER 1: 12–22

She blotted her copybook, sadly –
Queen Vashti refused rather badly
To attend the feast.
So the king dumped her – beast –
Then looked for another one, gladly!

ESTHER 2: 1–16

It so happened there was a girl
Who caught king's attention. A twirl
Was all that was needed
To ensure he heeded
Her beauty. He'd found some real pearl!

ESTHER 2: 17–23

He loved Esther more than the rest
And made her his queen. *'She's the best!'*
Said happy King A.
But it wasn't his day –
Her family put him to the test!

ESTHER 9

The secret of Esther came out
That she was Jewess, no doubt!
But Haman's vile plot
Was discovered. She got
The answer: *'All Jews' foes – wipe out!'*

JOB 1: 1–5

This Job was a rather nice chap –
All luxury fell in his lap!
But Satan devised
Tests that were well disguised –
Where Job might well give God the zap!

JOB 1: 6–19

A messenger came with bad news:
'Your family is dead, and the mews
Are full of dead cattle!
It's likely to rattle
The most righteous man in his shoes!'

JOB 1: 20–22

But Job took it all on the chin
He worshipped God, yet did not sin.
So Satan came running
With far greater cunning.
More tests were about to begin.

JOB 2

Job came out in boils everywhere
The thing that might make a man swear!
But sitting in ashes
Job scraped at his rashes,
And spent a week pulling his hair.

JOB 3

Eventually, Job spoke his mind
And nearly cracked up. But behind
Him each day there stood
His friends there, who were good
At comforting him. They were kind.

JOB 4–25

Eliphaz, Bildad, and Zophar
Kept visiting Job, the old gopher.
But what came across
Was that God was the Boss,
And Job never doubted His favour.

JOB 26–31

He wasn't convinced that what they
Told him was a help, come what may.
But Job knew that His
Own Redeemer still lives,
And that he'll stand at the last day!

JOB 42: 1–6

Job makes many clever remarks
Convinced that God loves him, he harks
To what God says here:
'I heard God with my ear
But now, I can see Him!' he barks!

JOB 42: 12–17

Eventually, God blessed his life
And Job died in happiness. Strife
Had not got him down.
'I will never disown
My God!' So he said to his wife!

PSALM 1

The man who delights in the Lord
Shall be like a tree grown abroad.
Its leaves will not wither,
Nor will the man dither –
For God leads the way with His Word.

PSALM 2

The nations rise up and fall down,
Their greatness is not all their own.
But those who trust God
Will be blessed, though His rod
Occasionally causes a frown!

PSALM 3

Despite all the problems around,
It's God's words that always abound.
He shields you – yes, you!
If you trust Him, it's true!
He blesses you! That's what we've found!

PSALM 4

At night, I will lie down in peace
Assured that God's love will not cease!
God answers my prayer
For I know that He's there.
In God, my trust's on the increase!

PSALM 5

Lead me, O Lord, to do right,
And make Your way plain in my sight.
For all who trust You,
Should rejoice as they do
Your will, Lord. There's no need to fight!

PSALM 6

Have mercy upon me, O Lord
And guide me, but not with Your sword!
My life is so bad
I become really sad
But try to keep faith with Your word!

PSALM 7

In You, Lord, do I put my trust!
I beg You to save me! I must
Not stray off Your path
Nor invite Your wrath!
I'll praise You for ever, or bust!

PSALM 8

How excellent, Lord, is Your Name!
The universe echoes Your fame!
From the weakest small child
To the power of the wild –
The whole earth proclaims You the same!

PSALM 9

I thank You Lord, with my whole heart,
To praise You for ever's my part!
The nations that shun You
You'll judge. And it's not new –
They are but men, so that's a start!

PSALM 10

The wicked man says there's no God!
He can't save himself on his tod!
Arise, Lord, and care
For the poor here and there.
Let wickedness rot in its pod!

PSALM 11

The Lord loves the upright man well,
The wicked can all burn in hell!
But righteousness brings
The way that He wants things
To be. That's the lesson to sell!

PSALM 12

It sometimes seems there's no one left
Who's godly. The world seems bereft
Of true faithful people
From temple to steeple
In this world's loom, from warp to weft.

PSALM 13

You won't forget me, Lord, for ever?
Our enemies reckon You'll sever
Your love from us here.
They rejoice at our fear!
But I'll not stop praising You! Never!

PSALM 14

The fool says there's no God. That's fact!
From heaven, the Lord thought, '*React!*'
'*Is anyone here*
Who fears God? The idea
Is far from our Covenant-pact!'

PSALM 15

Lord, what chap shall dwell in Your tent?
Your holy hill? Only one sent
To live a pure life,
With his children and wife.
Whoever does this is a gent!

PSALM 16

I trust You Lord. Keep me that way.
Preserve me, Lord – I'm here to stay!
But those who desert You
Are Godless, and hurt You,
But You are my compass all day!

PSALM 17

Don't let me slip down as I go,
Protect me, and be with me so.
Your wings' shadow hides me.
Let no lion chide me,
And I'll look for You, right – You know!

PSALM 18

My strength is in You, Lord – it's true!
Amaze me by all that You do!
This earth's myriad facets
Are some of Your assets –
If only the Godless ones knew!

PSALM 19

The heavens declare all God's glory,
And so does the earth. It's a story
That needs to be told
To all folk, young and old,
Sweeter than honeycomb could be!

PSALM 20

When times are bad, the Lord still hears you,
And helps you, when you feel He nears you!
Some folk trust in horses,
In chariots, and forces –
Not us! Your name shows we revere You!

PSALM 21

When the king trusts in God, that's so good!
You give him his heart's desire. Should
His enemies fight him,
Your hand will requite him,
And we'll sing Your praise! Yes, we would!

PSALM 22

My God, have You forsaken me?
It seems I'm abandoned – yes, me!
I'll still sing Your praise
For the rest of my days!
My family and I – we are for Thee!

PSALM 23

The Lord is my shepherd. He leads me
Beside the still waters He feeds me.
I walk without fear.
Rod and staff show He's near!
The feast, at His table, soon will be!

PSALM 24

Who shall ascend the Lord's hill?
With clean hands, pure heart, then he will
Find gates open wide.
Which king goes right inside?
King of glory! The Lord of hosts still!

PSALM 25

I lift up my soul unto Thee!
My foes are no problem to me!
My past life, forgive,
In Your way I will live!
I trust You lots, Lord – don't You see!

PSALM 26

O Lord, be my Judge. You can see
My trust has been always in Thee!
Wherever I've been
I have washed myself clean,
To proclaim the way You lead me!

PSALM 27

The Lord is my strength, and my light,
And salvation. When foes in sight
Encompass me round,
I just long to be found
With You. Don't forsake me! That's right!

PSALM 28

O Lord, hear my cry when I call
And hold me up, Lord, lest I fall.
Give those who are evil
Reward from the devil!
For joy, my heart dances! A ball!

PSALM 29

Give God what He's worth! Give the lot!
His power is amazing. He's got
The world in His hands,
Mightiness in all lands!
His blessing of peace comes soon! What!

PSALM 30

You finally rescued my soul
But sometimes, I doubted Your role!
When things went so wrong,
I called You, loud and long.
But now, Lord, You've made my life whole!

PSALM 31

I trust You, Lord! – I know You'll never
Forsake me, and I shall be ever
So grateful in praise,
Not deterred by the ways
Of the wicked, for their lives You'll sever!

PSALM 32

I own up. My life has not been,
Lord, up to Your standards. I've seen
What happens to men
Who sin so much. But then,
I'm going to live Your way! I'm keen!

PSALM 33

Rejoice, and sing praises with lute
And harp, and with ten strings, to boot!
The strength of a horse
Will not save me, of course –
But we trust You, Lord! Yes, You're cute!

PSALM 34

O taste, and see, just how the Lord is
So gracious to those who take orders
From God, not from men
Who are fickle. But then
You'll take us with You. All aboard! Yes!

PSALM 35

O God, confound those who do harm!
Cause their way of life to disarm!
So long as they live
Lord, Your vengeance will give
Them their due reward in their palm!

PSALM 36

The ways of the wicked are bad
So much so that they make You sad!
But in Your true light
We'll all see what is right,
By giving up evil! – You're glad!

PSALM 37

Fret not yourself for those who
Are ungodly – evil ones, too,
Whose ways are so bad
It's amazing they had
So much choice, to choose evil, or You!

PSALM 38

My health really has got me down
There's no good in me, on my own.
So come to me, quick
Lord, for I'm very sick!
You're God of my salvation!

PSALM 39

Lord, let me know when I shall die,
Lord, let me recover, so I
May be strong again,
And praise You! Yes! Amen!
At least, Lord, let me have a try!

PSALM 40

I sing with a new song today!
You're great, Lord! Hip, hip, hip, hooray!
Whoever deserts me
Lord, always preserve me!
And don't take too long! Help me! Hey!

PSALM 41

Whoever looks after the needy
You'll bless, Lord, and hope that it's speedy!
When I'm down in the dumps
Sure Lord, You'll man the pumps!
You'll help Lord! I hope I'm not greedy!

PSALM 42

My soul longs for You, like the hart
Desires to drink water. Apart
From You, Lord, I fail
But with You, Lord, I sail
Above waves and storms! – I take heart!

PSALM 43

Defend me, O God – You're so strong
Your light and Your truth – these I long
For, in Your holy house.
I've a heavy heart. Douse
My sadness! With harp, praise in song!

PSALM 44

Again, Lord, we pray You: defend
Us now, and when we reach the end
Of life as we know it.
You'll be there! You'll show it!
Arise, Lord, and help us amend!

PSALM 45

The king's coronation is grand,
Magnificent, best in the land!
The splendour is there,
While enhancing the fair,
With gladness and joy hand in hand!

PSALM 46

Our strength and our hope, when in trouble
Is in God, when seas rage and bubble.
He makes wars to cease
And He brings about peace!
Be still, then. God saves you from rubble!

PSALM 47

At the sound of the trump, God goes up.
A merry noise makes us all clap!
For God is the King
Over all the earth. Sing
His praises! Just like a young pup!

PSALM 48

Our God is so great, in the city
Of Sion, so proclaim this ditty:
Our God is the King
Of the universe! Sing
His praises well! Don't make them bitty!

PSALM 49

Some think that their wealth gives them power
And never guess it's their last hour!
Don't think you're immortal –
We all pass death's portal!
You can't take wealth with you, my flower!

PSALM 50

The sacrifice God wants of you
Is not that of animals. True!
Just give God due praise
And still follow His ways,
And that's where salvation is due!

PSALM 51

Lord, please turn Your face from my sin,
And make me a clean heart within!
Don't go far away,
But be near me all day.
My lips will praise You, Lord! – You win!

PSALM 52

So, look at the man who thinks he
Can do without God. He will see
That his way of life
Just brings trouble and strife!
But I trust God's mercy. That's me!

PSALM 53

The fool says, 'There's no God!' But then
That's typical thinking, of men!
We long for the day
When the Israelites say
'The Lord will deliver us!' – When?

PSALM 54

Please save me, O God, for the sake
Of Your name, and hear my prayer. Take
My heart, Lord, it's Yours!
I'll sing praise to Your doors!
Both when I'm asleep, and awake!

PSALM 55

When things get bad, Lord, You defend
Me. You have become a true friend!
I cast down my woes
At Your feet, Lord. It goes
To show how our lives can amend!

PSALM 56

Troubles surround me all day,
But my trust in God's here to stay!
I'm not understood
By my enemies! Would
That they trusted God, like I say!

PSALM 57

My foes are like arrows and spears
With tongues like sharp swords! But God hears
My song – thanks and praise
Reach to heaven! I raise
My hands to You Lord! Wipe my tears!

PSALM 58

Lord, sometimes my thoughts are not nice.
Consume all my foes in a trice!
There's nothing too bad
For my enemy! Cad
That he is! Lord – You know about vice!

PSALM 59

My foes grin like dogs, and they run
Around through the city. But one
Day, Lord, You'll give all
Of my foes, short or tall,
Their due reward! That should be fun!

PSALM 60

The nations around us are fearful,
But You help us not to be tearful!
You help us in trouble
And smite our foes double!
So make sure You give them a fist-full!

PSALM 61

O Lord, hear my prayer and my crying!
My heart is so heavy, I'm dying!
But under Your wing
I will praise You, and sing
Day by day! It's my foes I'm defying!

PSALM 62

God spoke once, and twice have I heard
That true power belongs to the Lord!
From Him comes my might
And my health, trust and sight,
So that nothing deflects from Your word!

PSALM 63

I call upon You, Lord, at dawn
You've been with me since I was born!
By day and by night
I remember You – right?
I need You, Lord, from night till morn!

PSALM 64

For those who have nothing to do
With You, Lord, show them something to
Make them well aware
That Your presence is there!
The man who is righteous trusts You!

PSALM 65

In Sion, O God, You are praised!
You hear all our prayers that are raised!
This intricate earth
You've made – gladness and mirth –
Even wheatfields laugh! We're just amazed!

PSALM 66

The whole world, with joy, worships You!
You've always looked after us, too!
Lord, hear all my prayer,
And yes –You're always there
For me. I can't help praising You!

PSALM 67

Be merciful, God, and us bless!
We'll praise You, God! Let all confess
Your name on the earth.
Let the nations give birth
To Your way of living – no less!

PSALM 68

Let God arise – and let Him scatter
Our foes – so that, nothing will matter
But singing Your praise
For the rest of our days –
And worshipping You, as we natter!

PSALM 69

I'm frightened and stuck in the mire!
I'm weary of crying! Enquire
From God, who will save you!
It's your life He gave you!
Let heaven and earth form a choir!

PSALM 70

Deliver me, Lord, now, in haste!
And grind all my foes to a paste!
But those who seek You
Will find joy – yes, it's true!
But help me, Lord – let's say You raced!

PSALM 71

O Lord, let me not be confused!
My trust in You won't be abused!
And when I am old –
Please wait until I've told
The next generations Your news!

PSALM 72

When Israel's king trusts in You, Lord
You'll bind nations up with a cord.
Let Israel be wealthy,
Its people all healthy,
And blessings from You will be heard!

PSALM 73

In Israel, God loves those who truly
Have clean hearts. But judgement comes duly
To those who are sinful –
They'll suffer a skinful
Of God's wrath. Let none be unruly!

PSALM 74

With You away, things have got worse
As if Israel's under a curse!
We've still got a pact
And we know how to act
As You want, and You'll reimburse!

PSALM 75

Impressed by Your wonderful work
We realise that we mustn't shirk
From fighting the foe.
We want all men to know
That Israel's God is no quirk!

PSALM 76

In Israel God's name is well known,
In Sion His tent and His throne.
We hold Him in awe
As we did years before.
He's wonderful, our God alone!

PSALM 77

I cry unto God. Does He hear me?
I wonder sometimes if He's near me?
His mercy – where is it?
We recall His visit
To Moses and Aaron by Red Sea!

PSALM 78

The history of Israel is fully
Recorded, but once more we duly
Read how God led us
With phenomenal fuss –
A powerful and patient God, truly!

PSALM 79

The heathen – they've entered the city –
Jerusalem's ruined! A pity!
The heathen with scorn
Ask us, 'Where's your God gone?'
They'll reap their reward soon! That's witty!

PSALM 80

We must learn from lessons gone past
To trust God. He'll turn us at last
To follow His ways –
So as long as we praise
Him! Again we'll be whole, and right fast!

PSALM 81

Sing merrily, make cheerful noise
With tabret, harp, lute, as our toys –
The trumpet as well –
With all these we will tell
How God once led Israel as boys!

PSALM 82

We look upon God as a judge
Defending the poor. He'll not budge
From justice for all.
Those who need Him may call,
And God will arise at a nudge!

PSALM 83

O God, keep not silence, but act
And let Israel's foes all be cracked!
Don't let them escape –
So they'll not make a jape
Of Your name – for it's Israel You backed!

PSALM 84

My soul longs to enter Your courts –
Like birds, building nests, all have thoughts
Their young to protect.
I would rather expect
To be Your doorkeeper, of sorts!

PSALM 85

Your graciousness pervades the land,
Lord. We are forgiven. You hand
Us righteousness, peace.
Truth and mercy increase,
You direct us all, as You planned!

PSALM 86

Among all the gods, there is no one
Like You, Lord. We bow down. There is none
Other god who'll do
Such great works, Lord, as You!
Your servant begs mercy be done!

PSALM 87

Sion's foundations are holy,
And God loves Jerusalem wholly!
The trumpets and singers
Eclipse Israel's slingers –
For all my fresh springs are in Thee!

PSALM 88

I'm miserable, Lord, as You know,
And my life is covered in woe!
In prison, I'm blind,
And my foes are behind
And around me – and I want to go!

PSALM 89

I sing of the Lord's kindness now
And glory in God's power, and how
His might is amazing
With nothing erasing
His record of victory. Wow!

PSALM 90

Our refuge, O Lord, in times past!
Before all creation, You'd cast
Us into a mould.
And although we grow old
We know You'll be there at the last!

PSALM 91

Whoever dwells under God's care
Need never fear anything there!
Whatever goes wrong
It'll not be for long –
And nothing is too hard to bear!

PSALM 92

At morning, it's time to sing praise
By music accompanied. Raise
Upon God your sights
And you'll find He delights
In worship you've done all your days!

PSALM 93

The Lord is robed up as a king
Who made the whole world – everything!
The waves of the sea
Still rage so horribly,
But holiness – God's peace will bring!

PSALM 94

O God, to whom vengeance belongs,
How much more can we take of wrongs
The heathen devise?
They say, 'Tush! – *no one spies*
Us!' Still – we praise God in our songs!

PSALM 95

O come, let us sing to the Lord
And worship Him. We can afford
To give Him His due
As He makes all things new –
So – sing today with one accord!

PSALM 96

Just sing to the Lord a new song!
Sing praises to Him all day long!
In holiness' beauty
Make worship your duty!
Let all heathen know they are wrong!

PSALM 97

The power of the Lord is so vast!
His strength and His might He has cast
All over the place!
So let no tribe or race
Ignore Him! For He's first, not last!

PSALM 98

Sing a new song to the Lord
His victory came with His sword!
In music and hymn
Let the whole world praise Him,
And floods and hills clap Him aboard!

PSALM 99

The Lord sits on high in the heavens.
Israel, at sixes and sevens
Discovered His voice
In the cloud. They rejoice
In Sion, as His law now leavens.

PSALM 100

O be joyful, all lands, and be glad
Be sure that the Lord, He is God!
He made us! He's pure!
Let His praises endure –
From father and son to granddad!

PSALM 101

Of Godliness, let me know more
And come to me, Lord, I implore!
But evil I'll shun,
Nor have wickedness – none!
I'll dwell with the faithful, for sure!

PSALM 102

O Lord, hear my crying, and prayer,
For I'm at rock bottom. Despair
Is my constant cry!
I'm not ready to die,
But You make the rules, and they're fair!

PSALM 103

My soul praises God. Like a dad
He takes care of us, though we're bad!
Our days, like the grass
Spring to life, then soon pass,
And we turn to dust. That's quite sad!

PSALM 104

God's power never ceases to thrill,
And birds, fish and animals still
Are part of His plan.
From the dust, creates man!
To praise Him for ever – I will!

PSALM 105

God's power was at maximum force
When Israel was set on its course
From Egypt. They went
Towards Canaan, and meant
To follow God's ways from the source!

PSALM 106

The people of Israel forgot
To follow their God. So they got
Themselves in such trouble
They had to pay double
For what they had done, and had not!

PSALM 107

In times of distress Israel's prayers
To God were like climbing steep stairs!
When God bailed them out
They took no time to shout
His praises. Then ditched Him for years!

PSALM 108

I'm ready, Lord, my heart is ready,
My faith in You grows deep and steady!
Your help in the past
Indicates it will last!
Our confidence makes us quite heady!

PSALM 109

Such wickedness round us is sadness,
And I don't approve of the badness
That goes on all round!
But as soon as they've found
Out the truth about You, Lord! That's gladness!

PSALM 110

King David was God's right-hand man,
But God's power was far greater than
One could have perceived
When David first believed
That he was a part of God's plan!

PSALM 111

The works of the Lord are so great,
And all His commandments relate
To His pact between
God and man. They are seen
As wisdom begins in man's state!

PSALM 112

The man who does what God wants will
Be blessed in abundance, and still
Will fear nothing bad
For God's word he has had –
But those who are wicked, He'll kill!

PSALM 113

From sunrise to sunset we'll praise
The name of the Lord, and we'll raise
Him high o'er the heathen
His glory o'er heaven,
With families happy for days!

PSALM 114

When Israel fled Egypt's land
God parted the Red Sea – that and
The waters of Jordan,
Defeated their cordon,
And hills skipped like sheep, hand in hand.

PSALM 115

The heathen are at it again!
'*So, where is your God?*' their refrain.
But their gods are dead
From the feet to the head!
While we praise the Lord – they're a pain!

PSALM 116

It's so good when God hears our prayers,
It uplifts your soul, ends your cares!
I walk now with Him
And thank God I'm not dim!
In the Lord's house I climb up the stairs!

PSALM 117

The nations should all join in praise,
The heathen should praise all their days!
God's kindness is there
More and more, yes, I swear!
The Lord's truth endures, and it stays!

PSALM 118

Those who fear the Lord, now confess
His mercy dispels strain and stress!
The builders erected
This stone once rejected –
He comes in God's name, and will bless!

PSALM 119: 1–8

Blessed are those who walk in
The way of the Lord, and don't sin!
With You, Lord, I gained
And my heart prays unfeigned –
You'll never forsake me! You win!

PSALM 119: 9–16

A young man cleans up his whole act
By keeping Your word, and Your pact!
For what You command
Is so clear. Let it stand –
And then You will see him react!

PSALM 119: 17–24

Your statutes are all that we need
So open our eyes, that we heed
The words that You say
Which I keep day by day!
Your servant, Lord – yes Lord, indeed!

PSALM 119: 25–32

My soul is stuck fast to the dust,
And so I pray, Lord, that I must
Seek truth and be clean
So You'll know where I've been,
With no more deception, I trust!

PSALM 119: 33–40

Teach me to learn, Lord, to stay
In touch with Your laws day by day.
Make my eyes to see
Your laws, not vanity,
And quicken me, Lord, in Your way!

PSALM 119: 41–48

I long for Your mercy and love
O Lord, send it down from above.
I lift up my hands
To receive Your commands,
To walk in Your ways – but don't shove!

PSALM 119: 49-56

At night I have thought of Your name.
I sing it by day – just the same!
The ungodly, though
Frighten me, Lord, and so
I don't want to play in their game!

PSALM 119: 57-64

I promised to keep all Your law
O Lord, but at midnight I saw
That my life is lacking
So don't send me packing!
Your mercy is what I implore!

PSALM 119: 65-72

I haven't lived pure as the snow,
But now I love You, so I know
Your law is worth more,
And I've learned to adore
Your statutes, Lord. Ain't that just so!

PSALM 119: 73–80

Your hands, Lord, have fashioned and made me
But I need to learn more, Lord. Aid me!
Your judgements are right
And Your law – my delight!
The wicked will want to evade me!

PSALM 119: 81–88

My soul, Lord, longs for Your salvation.
I long for Your comfort. My station –
Like bottle in smoke.
Foes say, *'What a sad bloke!'*
What can I do for reparation?

PSALM 119: 89–96

Your word, Lord, endures there for ever
In heaven. But Your word will never
Go far from my mind.
I'll not leave it behind,
Despite all my foes do. Whatever!

PSALM 119: 97–104

Lord, You know that I love Your law
I study it all day, and more!
Your laws make me wiser,
They're an appetiser –
Like honey gets stuck to my jaw!

PSALM 119: 105–112

Your word is a light for my feet,
A lantern, to light my paths. Greet
Me, Lord, in the dark
Where my enemies park
Their traps for me. Make them retreat!

PSALM 119: 113–120

I hate those who imagine evil,
Whose lives are controlled by the devil!
But 'stablish me fast
Lord, so I at the last
May stamp them out as a small weevil!

PSALM 119: 121–128

I deal with what's lawful and right,
But now it's affecting my sight!
I want to know more
Of Your law, but abhor
All false ways. Your law's a delight!

PSALM 119: 129–136

Your word gives such light to the simple,
It forms on my mouth like a dimple!
It makes my eyes cry
When bad people defy
Your laws, Lord. They're like a bad pimple!

PSALM 119: 137–144

Righteous are You, Lord! Be near me!
My zeal, Lord, has even consumed me!
I feel of no worth
Amongst people on earth,
But I'll keep Your laws, and I'll fear Thee!

PSALM 119: 145–152

I call with my whole heart, Lord, You know
I try to do what I should, e'en so
At morning I cry
Out for You, Lord. Be nigh,
And may Your commandments in me grow!

PSALM 119: 153–160

Deliver from adversity,
Health is far from the ungodly!
I have many foes,
Lord, yet none of them knows
That I'll never swerve from Your mercy!

PSALM 119: 161–168

Lord, princes without any cause
Have persecuted me. Your laws
I've loved. As for lies
Those I hate and despise!
I praise You each day! Yes, of course!

PSALM 119: 169–176

I beg You, Lord, deliver me
In order that Your praise should be
My song every day.
I've gone so far astray
Lord, like a lost sheep. Rescue me!

PSALM 120

I called on the Lord, and He heard me,
So troubled, what could He do for me?
If peace only came
When I mention its name!
My enemies just want to fight me!

PSALM 121

I lift up my eyes to the hills,
My help comes from God, despite ills.
While He keeps me safe
Sun and moon will not chafe.
My comings and goings God wills!

PSALM 122

I was glad when they said unto me,
'Let's visit the Lord's house. Let's see
Jerusalem's peace!'
And there, I'll not cease
To do good and be good. That's me!

PSALM 123

To thee, Lord, I lift up my eyes
Have mercy, for they all despise
Us. They are the wealthy,
And proud, but not healthy!
So Lord, we pray You – hear our cries!

PSALM 124

If Israel had not had the backing
Of God, we would not have sent packing
The soldiers of Pharaoh.
We took to the air – oh –
Like birds from the snare! It was cracking!

PSALM 125

Those folk, those whose trust is as solid
As Sion's mount – a fortress stolid –
Will stand fast for ever.
The wicked will never
Prevent peace in Israel. They're horrid!

PSALM 126

When Israel's freedom emerged
We laughed, cried with joy, joy that surged
Like seeds in a field
Which developed a yield,
And the reaper brought sheaves that converged!

PSALM 127

Unless it's the Lord God who builds it
The house will not last. Just believe it!
The kids you produce
Are like arrows shot loose,
And happy the man who won't doubt it!

PSALM 128

The chap who fears God will be blessed, and
He will eat the labours of his hand.
His wife, like the vine
Will have kids, maybe nine!
Prosperity, and peace, in our land!

PSALM 129

Some problems arose in time past,
But God was there, from first to last.
Like grass they were treated,
But not one was greeted
With *'Good luck in God's name!'* Surpassed!

PSALM 130

Out of the deep have I called Thee,
O Lord, hear my voice, I implore Thee.
My soul flees to You
Lord, – just say that it's true –
Redeem Israel. End of story!

PSALM 131

I'm humble, Lord, with no proud looks.
I'm not a high-flyer with books.
My soul knows no other
Than child with his mother,
And Israel's caught fast on God's hooks!

PSALM 132

To God David once made a vow –
His children would keep the pact. How?
In Sion, God blesses
All David's successes
By clothing his foes with shame now!

PSALM 133

It's good, and it's joyful, to dwell
Together in unity! Well –
It's like the anointing
Of Aaron, God's blessing
On Hermon in Sion is swell!

PSALM 134

You servants of God, you who stand
At night, praising God, lift your hand
And praise Him again
All your life! It is plain
In Sion, God's blessing is grand!

PSALM 135

Keep praising the Lord – the real One
Above other gods, not as done
In Israel's past
Pagan gods cropped up fast –
As lifeless as those who designed 'un!

PSALM 136

Give thanks to the Lord, fail Him never,
His mercy endures – yes, for ever!
The Exodus showed
How God's power really flowed,
Let no one from God Israel sever!

PSALM 137

By Babylon's waters, we wept
We hung up our harps, as we slept.
They said, '*Sing a song*
Of Sion!' It's so long
Since we left there. A song was inept.

PSALM 138

My whole heart is so full of praise!
Your truth, love and kindness amaze!
You hear when I call,
Pick me up when I fall.
You save me when trouble affrays!

PSALM 139

You know when I stand or sit down.
There's nowhere where You're not in town!
In heaven, You're there
As in depths of despair!
No foe competes with God's renown!

PSALM 140

The snares of the ungodly try
To trap me. O Lord, hear my cry!
You only avenge
All Your foes! And revenge
Is Yours. I'll still praise You on high!

PSALM 141

O Lord, keep me on the right track
And don't let me ever look back
On my evil ways.
Let my foes never raise
Their traps, Lord. Just give them the sack!

PSALM 142

My soul was in heaviness when
I cried to the Lord. Free me, then
I'll give thanks always
For the rest of my days –
And live as the most righteous men!

PSALM 143

I think of the past quite a lot,
And thank You for all that I got!
So teach me to do
All the things that please You!
My soul gasps, as if it's red hot!

PSALM 144

Defend me! In You, Lord, I trust!
My armour for battle won't rust
With You at my side!
I sing now – though I cried –
My friendship with You is a must!

PSALM 145

Let all speak of You, Lord, Your glory
And praise is a wonderful story!
We wait upon You
While You give us our due,
And scatter and rout the ungodly!

PSALM 146

As long as I live, I will sing
The praises of God. Everything
He does is so good –
Gives the hungry their food.
In Sion, our God shall be King!

PSALM 147

God builds up, and heals. And He knows
The names of the stars, and all grows
In His plan made clear
All things live for Him here –
Whether animals, or belles or beaux!

PSALM 148

The grandeur of God's world portrays
His power, and fantastic ways!
So all – young and old
See the story unfold,
And praise Him the rest of their days!

PSALM 149

O sing a new song, Israel!
Let children in Sion all tell
The world of their joy –
Every girl, every boy –
With tabret and harp, dance as well!

PSALM 150

God's holiness, greatness, and power
We praise, with loud music, each hour!
Harp, trumpet and lute,
Cymbals, dances and flute!
All who breathe – praise God, our Papa!

PROVERBS

Though Solomon wrote a good many,
The Proverbs emerged two-a-penny.
They give good advice
On what's nasty, or nice.
You can learn all by heart, or not any!

PROVERBS 25: 11–12

A word fitly spoken, we're told
Is like lots of apples of gold
In silvery baskets
Like wisdom in caskets –
So learn this before you get old!

PROVERBS 25: 21–22

If your enemy's hungry, it pays
To feed him! If thirsty, amaze
Him by your kind acts,
Quick, before he reacts!
So heap coals of fire on his ways!

PROVERBS 30: 15–16

You never can satisfy these:
The grave, and the childless! One sees
That earth without water
Is to son and daughter
A problem – like fire in the trees!

PROVERBS 30: 24–28

Four things that show wisdom: in turn
The ants and the rabbits both learn
To live on the land.
Locusts, lizards both stand
In hot places – and yet don't burn!

PROVERBS 31: 10–31

A virtuous woman is rare.
To find one, where would you look – where?
But find one whose word
Shows that she loves the Lord
And no one will with her compare!

ECCLESIASTES 1: 2

'Vanity!' – that's what he said –
The preacher's face grew rather red.
'There's nothing round here
Except vanity, dear!'
In which case, we should go to bed!

ECCLESIASTES 1: 15–18

The crooked thing can't be made straight.
In debt, there's not much to create!
In wisdom is grief.
And the man who's a thief
Will find just the same. Soon or late!

ECCLESIASTES 2: 18–19

I can't bear to think that my work
Is left for someone who will shirk.
If foolish or wise
Then he sees with his eyes
It's all vanity! That's no mean quirk!

ECCLESIASTES 3: 16–22

We know, whether good, whether bad,
That God judges us. We all had
The same love or lust,
And we all turn to dust!
It's all vanity! Sad or glad!

ECCLESIASTES 4: 9–12

Two chaps are far better than one,
In half the time get the job done!
With someone beside you
It's warm! Woe betide you
If you face a foe on your own!

ECCLESIASTES 9: 12

When fishes are caught in the net,
And birds in the snare, even yet
We can't know the day
When our life fades away.
If that's a surprise, then – get set!

ECCLESIASTES 12: 12

Of the making of books, there's no end.
And wisdom is learned, so amend
Your life while you may,
But don't read all the day –
Much study is wearisome, friend!

ECCLESIASTES 12: 13–14

This is our whole duty – we can
Fear God, and then work to His plan.
For God will judge all
That we do, so recall
That everything's vanity, man!

THE SONG OF SONGS

This – written by someone who knew
The tenderness Israel had, too –
The fighting and wars
Just showed one side. But pause
At this song of loveliness, do!

Whole chapters describe with affection
The beauty of each. In one section
Their love hits the heights!
They are smitten! The nights
And the days all their lovesickness mention!

THE SONG OF SONGS 8: 6–7

As a seal set me firm on your heart,
As a seal on your arm. But a part
Of life on this earth
Shows that love's strong as death!
No floods can drown love! That's a start!

ISAIAH

Isaiah is in three parts, so
I mention it, just so you know!
(Perhaps this best-quoted
Book ought to be noted –
For Jesus himself knew it! Oh!)

ISAIAH 1: 11–14

The Lord says, *'I've had quite enough
Of animal sacrifice! Tough!
I want no more incense
So please make no pretence –
Just don't mix the smooth with the rough!'*

ISAIAH 1: 18

'Come, *reason together, my friends,*'
The Lord says. So let's make amends!
With scarlet sins, know
That they'll be white as snow!
Not red, but like wool, when sin ends!

ISAIAH 2: 4

When we walk the way that God wants,
The nations will find His peace blunts
Their swords into ploughs,
And for pruning the boughs
Their hooks will be what spears were once!

ISAIAH 2: 19

Some time in the future, there'll be
A Day of the Lord – just you see –
When men out of fear
Will hide there, and hide here –
From the glory of His majesty!

ISAIAH 3: 16–26

While the daughters of Zion are haughty
And mince around, ever so naughty –
God's judgement will come
And affect every home!
It's likely to be their last sortie!

ISAIAH 4–5

It's going to be terrible for
Some people, with such woes galore!
The sea will be roaring
With people imploring
The Lord to pass by their front door!

ISAIAH 6: 1–8

The year when King Uzziah died
I saw the Lord enthroned, and sighed
As seraphim lowly
Sang 'Holy – yes, holy –
The Lord of hosts's holy!' they cried.

ISAIAH 6: 9–13

Go, tell all the people. They hear,
But understand not! – It's so clear
They see, but they don't!
In their hearts they just won't
Turn round, and be healed! Dear, oh dear!

ISAIAH 7: 14

A sign from the Lord Himself will
Tell you that a young girl – a thrill –
Will bring forth a son
And He's truly the One!
His name will be Immanuel!

ISAIAH 8: 14–15

The Lord is a sanctuary – true!
A stumbling block and snare, if you
Ignore His commands!
It's just what God demands!
But woe betide you till you do!

ISAIAH 9: 2, 6–7

The people who walked in the dark
Have seen a great light, and remark
That God's name is great!
A mere child will translate!
No end to His peacefulness – mark!

ISAIAH 11: 1–5

From Jesse's house a branch shall grow
With wisdom and knowledge, you know,
With counsel and might
And the fear of God – right!
(It's Jesus he means!) There you go!

ISAIAH 11: 6–9

The wolf now at peace with the lamb
The leopard and kid – just like jam –
Will mingle together
With calf, lion – whatever –
A child leads the whole lot! Yes, ma'am!

ISAIAH 25: 8–9

The Lord God will wipe away tears
And end the reproach of the years,
As He lifts up the veil
From the nations' travail,
'We've waited for this day, My dears!'

ISAIAH 28: 16

In Zion, the foundation stone
Becomes so important. There's none
So precious as that
Cornerstone! It's the mat
Upon which the nations' feet run!

ISAIAH 32: 15

In due time, the Spirit will pour
Upon us from on high – and more!
In the desert, springs fruit!
From the wilderness root
A forest shall grow up! Encore!

ISAIAH 35: 4–7

Your God will come one day, and then
The blind will see, deaf will hear! Men
Will leap, though they're lame
And will sing the Lord's name!
And streams in the desert will run!

ISAIAH 35: 8–10

A highway called 'Holiness' there
Will be, for the ransomed ones, where
No sadness or sorrow
But gladness! Tomorrow
Will be Zion's joy, I declare!

ISAIAH 40: 1–2

'Comfort my people, and speak,'
Says God, 'and please tell them this week
Their warfare is over,
From sins now recover!
It's true, both for strong as for weak!'

ISAIAH 40: 3–8

A voice cries out, 'Make the way straight
For God! Level mountains, and wait
To see God's true glory
And then tell the story
Because this comes from the Lord! Right!'

ISAIAH 40: 9–11

Tell Zion! Tell Judah! 'He'll come –
The Lord God! The lambs in His arm
He'll so gently carry.
This shepherd won't tarry,
But He'll keep you safe from all harm!'

ISAIAH 40: 18–24

To whom will you liken God, then?
With what can you compare Him? Men?
With idols of metal?
With workmen's fine fettle?
You can't compare God! D'ya ken!

ISAIAH 40: 31

Those will – who upon the Lord wait –
Renew all their strength, and not faint!
Like eagles they'll fly,
Run, and not be weary!
They'll walk with God, at a fresh gait!

ISAIAH 42: 1–7

My Servant, in whom I delight
Shall be to the Gentiles a light!
He'll open blind eyes,
And in prison surprise
All, as He leads them out of their plight!

ISAIAH 45: 8

Drop down from above, from the skies
And let heavens open. Your eyes
Will openly see
Your salvation from me,
With righteousness too, as the prize!

ISAIAH 50: 6

I then gave my back to the smiters,
My cheeks to those there who were fighters,
Who plucked off my hair,
Spat at me without care,
And made me endure this! The blighters!

ISAIAH 52: 7

How beautiful there are the feet
Of those, who, with good tidings greet
All – nephew and niece –
And who publish such peace:
'*Our God reigns in Zion! Let's meet!*'

ISAIAH 53: 3–5

He was so despised and rejected
Of men, and by sorrows affected.
He was wounded for us –
Our iniquities, plus
By His healing stripes, we are healed.

ISAIAH 53: 7–9

Led like a lamb tied up, penned,
In silence, no words to defend –
For our sins He died,
And His grave was beside
Wicked men's. Innocent to the end!

ISAIAH 55: 6–12

So, while you can find the Lord, seek
Him! You'll be led forth with the peak
Of the mountains and hills
Which will break forth in thrills
Of singing, and clapping, all week!

ISAIAH 56: 7–8

My house shall be called 'House of Prayer'
For all nations. Everyone there –
The strangers as well
As yourselves, Israel –
Will worship the true God, all year!

ISAIAH 61: 1–2

God's Spirit is on me! Hooray!
I preach the good news, that I may
Uplift broken-hearted,
Free captives – once started,
The year of the Lord's here to stay!

JEREMIAH 1: 1–9

As a child, Jeremiah said, '*I
Can't speak, Lord, in public!*' '*But why?*'
Said God, '*You will go,
And what you'll need to know,
I'll tell you! – So go on, and try!*'

JEREMIAH 5: 31 – 6: 14

False prophets in Israel mislead
The people, and wallow in greed!
They falsely cry, '*Peace!*'
Blatant lies, full of grease –
And nobody cares much, indeed!

JEREMIAH 11: 6–8

Young Jerry pitched into a few
Who centralised worship, but knew
That God wants the heart
For His law. Just a part
Of Jerusalem's city won't do!

JEREMIAH 11: 18–23

Resistance to Jerry proved strong
With arguments frequent and long.
Jerusalem nobs
Said '*We'll all lose our jobs!*'
'*It's your fault!*' said Jerry – '*You're wrong!*'

JEREMIAH 20: 7–18

Poor Jerry became laughingstock
As folk came along just to mock
Him day after day
As they passed on their way.
'*Lord, why put my head on the block?*'

JEREMIAH 23: 5–8

The Lord said, 'One day soon, I'll raise
Of David, a righteous branch. Gaze
On His wise, long reign
When all Israel will gain
Their own land!' Now that's worth some praise!

JEREMIAH 23: 15–18

Sometimes, the prophets would seem
To have special knowledge: 'I dream
This, that or the other!'
We have to ask whether
Their dreams are their own, or God's, scheme?

JEREMIAH 31: 10–14

The picture of Zion's great fun –
When all Israel's tribes join as one,
And dance in the street –
Young and old, they all meet
In joy, now that sorrow's clean gone!

JEREMIAH 31: 33

'My Covenant's a pact that will be
Engraved on your hearts, Israel! See –
I'll be your true God,
So you won't think it odd –
For you'll be My people!' Yippee!

JEREMIAH 32: 17

O Lord, by Your power You made
Both heaven and earth. I'm afraid
I've got to admit
That Your power shows me it
Finds nothing that it can't pervade!

JEREMIAH 36

Once, Jehoiakim, Israel's king
Told Baruch to write up a thing
He later destroyed.
So Baruch, still employed
By Jerry, just wrote it again!

JEREMIAH 38: 7–13

Jeremiah was put down a pit
When Ebed-melech said that it
Was wrong. *'Come here men*
We'll pull him out again!'
Such friendship helped Jerry a bit!

LAMENTATIONS

In Zion sat Baruch, sat he
About year five six o BC.
He wrote Lamentations,
A sad tale of nations –
(Not by Jeremiah, maybe!)

It's quite chock-a-block with the woes
That Israel faced, against their foes.
He mourns for the Zion
He once knew, but iron
Is not quite like gold, and it shows!

EZEKIEL 1: 1–9

Ezekiel slept, and he dreamed
That Israel was not as it seemed.
His visions were stark
Like a storm in the dark,
When the weirdest of imagery teemed!

EZEKIEL 1: 10–28

Creatures with wings and strange face –
A man, eagle, ox, wheels that race,
And fire where they went!
What this dream could have meant
Was puzzling, like holes within lace!

EZEKIEL 2

The Spirit came into him finally,
Ezekiel realised eventually
That he was the one
God had picked to become
A prophet in Israel, convincingly.

EZEKIEL 3

The Spirit uplifted me, and
A rushing wind said, '*Understand*
In this place, the glory
Of the Lord! Your story
Will take you to a foreign land.'

EZEKIEL 4

To make the point, old Ezek lay
On left side for many a day.
And then on his right –
Forty days at the sight
Of Israel and Judah *mauvais!*

EZEKIEL 5

And then Ez cut some of his hair
And weighed it in three, then and there.
He burnt it to show
How the nation would go,
But no one much bothered to stare!

EZEKIEL 9

Not very long after, in Zion
The Spirit whisked me there to spy on
The evil being done
By almost every one –
Not quite the folks God could rely on!

EZEKIEL 11

In all this, God softened and said
'I'll give them a new heart! Instead
Of stone, let's have flesh
So that they walk afresh,
And I'll be their God till they're dead!'

EZEKIEL 13

Folk are being seduced by false words,
Proclaiming there's peace, when it's swords!
Don't paper the cracks
While they don't guard their backs,
Catastrophe's coming, you nerds!

EZEKIEL 34

'A shepherd,' the Lord said, 'I'll be
And seek out My sheep – just you see!
In pastures so green
Is where My sheep have been,
And I'll care for them! They're with Me!'

EZEKIEL 37

A valley of bones, full and dry,
But can these bones live? 'Let me try!'
The Lord said, and blew
His breath over them – true –
Inspired with new life – they said, 'Hi!'

EZEKIEL 43

In vision, I'm now at the gate
Of eastern Jerusalem. Wait! –
The Spirit led me
To God's glory, you see –
Restored Temple this shall soon be!

DANIEL 1: 1–2

Nebuchadnezzar the king
Of Babylon formed a great ring
Around Zion's city
And said, '*What a pity!* –
To Babylon, now, you I bring!'

DANIEL 1: 3–6

Neb wanted some bright young men who
Were skilful in knowledge. '*You'll do*'
Azariah and Daniel
Hananiah, Mishael' –
Neb gave them new names, as you do!

DANIEL 1: 7

So now, Belteshazzar was Dan,
And Az was Abednego, man!
And Han was called Shadrach
While Mishael was Meshach,
All part of old King Nebbie's plan!

DANIEL 2: 1–13

King Neb set a task. His wise men
Must guess what he dreamed about, then
Tell him what it meant
Or their heads would be rent
From their bodies! But they did'na ken!

DANIEL 2: 17–35

So Daniel prayed hard, and up came
Solution to old Nebbie's dream.
An image of gold
Just fell down, so we're told,
And into a mountain became!

DANIEL 2: 36–46

Old Nebbie asked, *'What does this mean?'*
Then Daniel explained, *'It is seen
That one day, there'll be
God's great kingdom, you see,
Which never will end! Tell the queen!'*

DANIEL 2: 48

Neb promoted Dan straightaway,
And gave him the governor's pay,
As he oversaw
All of Babylon, for
King Nebbie. And that made Dan's day!

DANIEL 3: 1–7

An image of gold King Neb made
And said, *'When the music is played,*
All must bow down low!
If you don't, you will go
In a furnace so fiery – you'll fade!

DANIEL 3: 8–22

Inevitably, three refused
And so did a lot of the Jews.
So Neb chucked them in
To the furnace. A grin
Came over his face. *'I'm amused!'*

DANIEL 3: 23–30

But Shad, Mesh, and Abednego
From fire emerged unscathed. *'Hello!'*
Neb was so impressed
He said they were the best –
And promoted them all in a row!

DANIEL 4

More dreaming of grandeur Neb had,
Which Dan understood. He was glad –
So much so, that he
Led King Neb to agree
That Dan's God was best! *'Well done, lad!'*

DANIEL 5: 1–4

Belshazzar's feast – plenty of wine
And women, and song. By design
He used temple vessels –
(Such sacrilege hassles!) –
But thought, *'This is great! It's just fine!'*

Daniel 5: 5–7

A moment arrived, somewhat sinister
When fingers wrote words on the plaster.
Bel came over faint,
'What do these letters paint?
Interpret these words for your master!'

Daniel 5: 8–28

Again, Daniel came to the rescue!
'You're weighed in the balances, but you
Are found sadly wanting!
Mene Tekel Upharsin
Your kingdom is long overdue!'

Daniel 5: 29 – 6: 16

That night King Belshazzar was slain!
So Darius assumed the reign.
'Put Dan to the test!'
He cried, *'and all the rest!*
In a lions' den they will remain!'

DANIEL 6: 17–24

No law of the Persians and Medes
Could ever be changed. So then pleads
Daniel to God. *'We need*
Your help to be freed!'
By lions unharmed, Dan succeeds!

DANIEL 6: 25–28

Successful, Daniel made King Dar
Proclaim decree: *'Men near and far*
Will worship the true
God – that's Daniel's – who
Delivered him from lions' power!'

DANIEL 7: 1–8

It was Dan's turn to dream, not the king's!
The first was a lion with wings,
The second a bear,
And a leopard was there,
And a beast, ten horns, man's eyes and things!

DANIEL 7: 9–14

In clouds in the heavens appeared
A son of man – widely revered –
The Ancient of Days,
To whom all men give praise –
Whose kingdom for ever endured!

DANIEL 7: 15–18

Interpreting dreams wasn't easy
In fact, it made Dan feel quite queasy:
'Four kingdoms remain,
But the Most High will gain
The whole world – which for Him's easy peesy!'

DANIEL 7: 19–28

This vision upset Dan a bit –
Unsure what he might make of it!
'This kingdom is given
To the saints in heaven
Who'll serve and obey, as is fit!'

DANIEL 8: 1–14

A second dream Dan had, please note,
A ram charged a poor billy-goat!
The billy-goat won,
'Aha – now we'll have fun!'
Said Dan! This is then what he wrote:

DANIEL 8: 15–27

Gabriel, the angel, made clear
To Daniel. *'The ram – this one dear –*
Represents all
Medes and Persians, their fall –
As Greece conquers everything here!'

DANIEL 9–12

So what Daniel dreamed as a piece
Came true. Persia yielded to Greece!
What seemed like a trick
This apocalyptic,
Summed up Israel's yearning for peace!

HOSEA 1

Hosea had had a bad marriage.
His wife had gone off like a carriage!
As unfaithful wife
He compared Israel's life
As a nation. Would this make God savage?

HOSEA 3

Despite being deserted by them
God said, 'It is true, there's no phlegm
At all on My part –
But there's love in My heart!
Your wife should be prized like a gem!'

HOSEA 6: 6

To make the point, God said, 'Look – I
Don't want sacrifice, but mercy!
To know God is more
Than burnt offerings, for
That's what sort of God I am! Hi!'

JOEL 1

The son of Pethuel, called Joel,
Had warnings for Israel. Well, well!
'The locusts will come!'
He said, *'and you'll be dumb*
If you don't repent quickly, Israel!'

JOEL 2: 1–2

'It's *going to be horrible gloom*
With clouds and thick darkness and doom!
For the Day of the Lord
Will arrive like a sword!
Prepare yourselves now! Flee to whom?'

JOEL 2: 12–14

The Lord says, *'Turn now, even now!*
Rend hearts, not your garments!' God's slow
To anger! But note
His compassionate vote
Is merciful, gracious! And how!

JOEL 2: 28-29

'My Spirit I'll pour out on all.
Your daughters and sons will enthral
In prophetic team,
While your old men will dream,
Your young men, with visions, will fall.'

JOEL 2: 30-32

'The sun shall be turned into dark,
The moon to blood, with fire and smoke
Before the day dawns,'
'It will be,' – Joel warns –
'The time when you know God will hark!'

JOEL 3: 9-16

'Let all men of war listen here.
Turn pruning hook now into spear!
Beat ploughshares to swords
You must listen – My words,'
Says God – 'are the things you must fear!'

Amos 1: 1

A shepherd called Amos in Judah
Kept fig trees. He lived in Tekoah.
But God sent him north
Telling him, '*You speak forth*
Against Jereboam, the rotter!'

Amos

King Jerry had set up an idol –
A golden calf. This was a trial
For Amos, so brave
Proclaimed that God would save
The righteous alone, not the vile!

The traders aren't good when they cheat!
Dishonesty is never sweet!
To sacrifice daily
But not repent, really –
A very strange use of raw meat!

The first chap in Testament Old
To write, was young Amos the bold.
The priest at Bethel
In the king's pay as well
Said, 'Quit, Amos, *now you've been told!*'

In warning folk, Amos had meant
To steer Israel back to repent
Of evils they'd done,
Or they'd find – every one –
That God would be fierce in judgement!

AMOS 7: 7–8

The Lord, in a vision, showed me
A plumb line beside a wall. *'See*
This line, Amos? It
Will test Israel. Sit
A moment. What will its fate be?'

OBADIAH

In one chapter only, we see
Obadiah, steward was he.
As Jezebel raves,
He hid prophets in caves,
A hundred of whom he set free!

JONAH 1: 1–2

God contacted Jonah: 'Convey
My message at once! Nineveh
Is wicked. Don't moan –
You must go on your own!
Whatever you do, don't delay!'

JONAH 1: 3

But Jonah had no plans in mind
To go there. Instead he would find
Excuses galore –
Visit some other shore,
And leave Nineveh well behind!

JONAH 1: 4–15

A tempest blew up, and the ship
Fair broke into pieces. The trip
Was now a disaster.
'We'll just have to cast ya
Right into the sea for a dip!'

JONAH 1:17

It happened that a great big fish
Was also en route to Tarshish.
It saw Jonah wallowing
And couldn't help swallowing
Him up! _'This is some tasty dish!'_

JONAH 2

By night and by day Jonah prayed
To God. _'I'd much rather have stayed_
On dry land,' he said.
Three days after, not dead
The fish spewed him up! May Day! Aid!

JONAH 3: 1–4

A second time, God told him to
Go to Nineveh. *'Tell them, do –*
Repent this same day
As there's no other way!'
So Jonah obeyed this time. Phew!

JONAH 3: 5–10

The king and the people prayed hard,
And fasted, with Jonah on guard,
When God showed His pity
By sparing the city,
But Jonah had played his last card!

JONAH 4: 5–10

He sat 'neath a gourd in the shade
Which withered next day. A tirade
From Jonah came then.
'How could God forgive men
Whom Israel their enemy made?'

JONAH 4: 11

So God had to teach Jonah quickly
A lesson that made him quite sickly.
'It pays to show pity
E'en to a bad city!'
Said God. Exit Jo, feeling prickly!

MICAH 1: 1–2

To Micah, the Morashtite came
The word of the Lord, just the same
As that of Isaiah,
Of Amos, Hosea –
To Samaria – Jerus'lem.

MICAH

Predicting that both places would
Be destroyed for what was not good –
Their bad evil ways
To the poor there, betrays
How badly their leaders had stood!

MICAH 6: 7–8

The Lord said, 'I'm fed up with rams
As sacrifice, or babes in prams,
Or rivers of oil!
What I want from your soil
Is justice and mercy! Sirs! Ma'ams!'

NAHUM

From Nahum the Elkoshite, three
Short chapters contain prophecy.
About six one two
Nineveh – yes, it's true –
Was captured by Babylon, see!

NAHUM 2–3

Assyrian capital city
Yes, Nineveh, town without pity,
So cruel to those
Who were Nineveh's foes,
'You'll be destroyed!' was Nahum's ditty.

HABAKKUK

In Judah, Habakkuk thought hard
How God could use foes who were tarred
With wickedness such
As the Chaldaeans! Much
Distress caused to Israel! Some bard!

He prayed at great length, and with style,
To God. And his answer came while
He realised one day
That all nations would pay –
As God judges all, good or vile!

ZEPHANIAH

Of Cushi, Zephaniah, son
Warned people in Judah to shun
Their idols and magic.
Their worship was tragic,
With God's laws infrequently done!

But those who came back to God would
Enjoy the future as they should!
The darkness and gloom
Would evaporate! Boom!
And life would be brighter, and good!

HAGGAI

In two chapters, Haggai's distaste
For those in Jerusalem who faced
Such comfort and ease
In their houses! 'But, *please* –
Look hard at the temple – now disgraced!'

HAGGAI 2: 18

'*Let's build it again, even better*'
Said Haggai, bold to the letter!
'*The foundation stone*
Has been laid. Now don't moan,
But – *let's get it built!*' A go-getter!

ZECHARIAH 1: 1–17

In five twenty BC, the Jews
Returned to Jerusalem. 'Lose
Heart? That you must not!'
Zech said, 'What we have got
To do here is proclaim *good news!*'

ZECHARIAH 2–8

He spent time encouraging men
To rebuild the Temple and then
To start to be proud
Of what freedom allowed –
'Yes – *a bright future follows! Amen!*'

ZECHARIAH 9: 9

O daughter of Zion, rejoice!
Your king comes to you. He's your choice!
Though, riding so slowly
Upon an ass, lowly,
With salvation, justice, and poise!

ZECHARIAH 12: 10

'On David's house, and Zion's face.
I'll pour supplication and grace.
And those who pierced me
Will look closely, and be
As mourners who walk at slow pace.'

ZECHARIAH 13

'In those days, the shepherd will flee
And sheep will be scattered, you'll see!
But one day, you know
Living waters shall go
Out from Zion's city!' Yippee!

MALACHI

Malachi – that was his name
Means 'messenger.' He would proclaim
The coming Messiah!
No message was higher,
And that was Mal's one claim to fame!

MALACHI 1: 11

From sunrise right up to sunset
God's name shall be great, even yet
Among Gentiles' land
In all places, where stand
The offerings of incense. He's great!

MALACHI 3: 1–3

'My messenger prepares my way
But who here may abide the day
He comes? Who shall stand
When with fire in His hand
He purifies silver? Who may?'

MALACHI 4: 4–6

'Behold, I will send down to you
Elijah the prophet, he who
Will foretell the day
Of the Lord, and hearts may
Turn to one another!' Tood'loo!

THE APOCRYPHA

1 Esdras

Describing their history, the Jews
Returned from exile with the news:
'Darius the king
Will support rebuilding
Our temple – to give him his dues!'

1 Esdras 3

King Darius first posed a riddle
To bodyguards. Three, in the middle
Debated with king,
'What's the strongest? What thing?
A puzzle, chaps!' Hey, diddle diddle!

The four options put to those men
Were wine, or the king, or women,
Or truth? What a choice!
But the king heard the voice
Of Zerubbabel once again.

'The answer is truth!' he replied!
'I really agree!' Darius sighed!
So, as you have won
The prize, you are the one
Who'll go back to Zion with pride!

'Go – rebuild your temple today!
And I'll help you do it! I'll pay
As much as it takes
There are no higher stakes!
Let it be Jerusalem's day!'

2 ESDRAS

Events of their nation, this book
In summary form. Take a look!
From Exodus to
The Apocalypse, you
May read up what course history took!

TOBIT

In Tobit, the author writes on
Conditions in old Babylon.
The Jews there in exile
Were urged to be faithful
To God, whom they rested upon!

He recommends a way of life
Encompassing virtue, not strife!
'It's good to give alms
As a habit. It charms
The needy, as well as your wife!'

Old Tobit went finally blind
But Raphael the angel, so kind
Helped cure him, we learn
And on Sarah's return
From a demon, in marriage they bind!

In chapter five, verse sixteen, we
Read he had a faithful doggy!
Its favourable mention
Is no mean invention –
Unique in the Bible! Wowee!

JUDITH

In Judith, a novel we find –
One of an historical kind.
The hatred comes through
Of the Gentiles – a Jew
Would try to rid them from his mind!

Its orthodox stance clearly shows
That faith in God overcomes woes.
But Nebuchadnezzar
Failed in his attempts there
To win Jews' support 'gainst his foes!

So Judith, a widow so young
And beautiful, sings them a song.
To God she gives praise
As she tries to erase
The Jews' fear of anyone strong.

ESTHER

Unique in the Bible, we read
No mention of God here! But heed
The Feast of Purim
Which to Jews meant a hymn
To deliver them from death indeed!

WISDOM OF SOLOMON

An Alexandrian Jew wrote
This book, as if, by him of note –
King Solomon. But
The words that he put
Down here, were much later, I quote!

From virtuous living to the
Choice of friends, this book seems to be.
With practical details
On learning, it retails
The fear of the Lord, don't you see!

The fear of the Lord is the start
Of wisdom, which springs from the heart,
Or is it the head?
Like what Solomon said!
Just read it, to feel you take part!

Ecclesiasticus

Read Ecclesiasticus, when
You'll know all about famous men
Who strove after wisdom!
If only CD ROM
To them was available then!

Wisdom, a female form takes –
A rather nice idea that makes
A man pay attention!
For by her instruction
A man, who sleeps, finds he awakes!

It tells what will make a man glad
As well as what makes a man sad.
A woman or man
Who is bad in life can
Find some wise words here! Yes, by gad!

From chapter four four he lists men
So famous in Israel! Then –
From Abraham to
BC one thirty two,
He shows wisdom's effects! Amen!

BARUCH

This book, at first sight by a Jew
Had Christian influence too –
Put in some years later
By a Greek translator –
Maybe not Baruch. Wonder who?

In chapter six, we have a letter
Which might have come very much better
From Jeremiah
Yes, the prophetic sire –
The one whose book's in the OT, Sir!

It harks back to when the Chaldeans
Invaded Jerusalem, aeons
Ago! Yes, enquire –
They destroyed it with fire!
A sad time! Of praising, no paeans!

THE SONG OF THE THREE HOLY CHILDREN

In far greater detail, we see
The plight of those men, yes, all three
Who walked in the dire
Fiery furnace, the fire
Didn't touch them! As Daniel says, see!

In sixty-eight verses, we're told
Of those three, the ones who were bold
In facing disaster!
But praising their Master
They emerged unscathed! Pure as gold!

From verse thirty-five, comes the nicety –
Familiar song – Benedicite!
It prays that all things
Should praise God, and it sings
That His mercy endures for eternity!

THE HISTORY OF SUSANNA

In sixty-four verses this lass –
Accused of a crime that was crass!
But Daniel's wisdom
Delivered this woman
From rumours that she'd made a pass!

It happened on one sunny day
That Susie went out just to play
Naked, in her garden
Where, unseen by two men,
She started to wash herself. Hey!

Those two men approached her alone
And got her down there on her own.
'You lie with us here!
If not, we'll say we hear
That you planned it all, so don't moan!'

But Susie screamed with a loud voice!
Alerted the guards. '_What's the noise,_
Susanna?' She cried
'_It's these men!_' and replied –
'_They threatened to rape me! The goys!_'

At this Daniel came to the court
'_I represent Susan! Her sort_
Is innocent! You
Know that she's a good Jew!'
Death came to those two men they caught!

BEL AND THE DRAGON

Two stories attached to the text
Of the Book of Daniel. It vexed
Him about the lies
That were told. '_I despise_
All falsehood!' Dan said. What came next?

There was a huge image called Bel
Where people brought food – lovely smell!
Each day it appeared
That the food disappeared –
(The priests knew where to, very well!)

But folk thought that Bel always ate it
Till Dan said, 'Look – *these priests, they get it!*'
Exposing their ruse
Became such headline news,
That Bel was destroyed, to Dan's credit!

The priests too, were put to death, and
Dan's fame spread throughout all the land!
The next story, though
Is a nasty one, so –
It might make your hair on end stand!

Derived from a Semitic myth
A dragon seized Dan in its teeth!
But Dan won king's vote
When he rammed down its throat
Some balls of fat, hair and black pitch!

The people, enraged that he'd won
Persuaded the king, that for fun
Young Daniel should be
Caged with lions, not three
But seven! And so it was done!

But right in the nick of time, Dan
Was saved by Habbakkuk, who ran
Amazingly too
From Judaea! But you
Believe it or not – yes, you can!

THE PRAYER OF MANASSES

Put into words, just as if he
Manasses, the king, wrote them. Did he?
This short book of prose
Is a prayer that goes
Quite movingly, to God Almighty!

The scene's set in Babylon where he
Was captive, in exile. So you see
That Judah's King
Manasses had to sing
God's praises, and yet ask God's mercy!

1 MACCABEES

In roughly one hundred BC
This book was compiled, so that we
May read what it seems
Like, beneath the regimes
Of Greek rule, for Jews like MacBee!

Antiochus Epiphanes,
Exterminates Jews there like fleas!
Obsessed with Greek culture
He swoops like a vulture
With Jerusalem on its knees!

1 MACCABEES 1: 20–24

The temple was first on his list.
He stole from it, and with his fist
In BC one-six-eight
He said, 'Exterminate
All those Jews, who my rule resist!'

1 MACCABEES 2

The history of his deeds of evil
Are really quite unbelieveable!
But young Mattathias
Had none of this bias
Towards pagan gods, or the devil!

1 MACCABEES 2: 15–22

One day, under pressure – 'Conform!
Or you'll pay the price! – It's the norm!'
But Matty resisted
'I won't!' – he protested!
And so a rebellion did form!

1 MACCABEES 2: 23–26

One day, in the temple, Matt slew
A worshipper there, yes – a Jew –
Obeyed pagan orders,
In Israel's borders!
So Matt killed the officer, too!

1 MACCABEES 3–15

On Matt's death, his son Judas rose –
As fearless, as the record shows.
In turn, came Jonathan
And then brother Simon –
A merciless lot, to their foes!

1 MACCABEES 6: 43–47

A strange tale of Eleazar:
He charged on an elephant. *'Aargh!'*
He said, as with fear
He lunged deep with his spear,
And killed the poor beast through its rear!

1 MACCABEES 16

But they at the last met their ends,
No more was Zion in their hands!
The Maccs' bold uprising
Was really surprising!
Greek rule now, once more, is what stands!

2 MACCABEES

The second war of Maccabees,
Was equally bold, if you please!
Now Antiochus
Has been slain, then for us
The temple's ours! Worship at ease!

Once more, subterfuge ruled the day
And intrigues increased all the way.
But the day came when
The Greeks Rule, OK! Then
Israel had no more to say!

One incident shows pain and stress
A woman endured. 'No? Or yes?'
Her tormentors said –
'You'll bow low, or you're dead!' –
She'd not submit under duress!

To make her crack up, they killed seven
Sons in front of her, who were even
Scalped, and fried alive,
Butchered. She said, 'Look, I've
A man's strength! I'll see you in heaven!'

And so it goes on to the last!
Some history of Israel is cast
Within the Apocrypha
So that we know of the
Problems and triumphs they passed!